Surviving The Workplace While Keeping Your Soul Intact

Surviving The Workplace While Keeping Your Soul Intact

C. K. Gold

Writers Club Press
San Jose New York Lincoln Shanghai

Surviving The Workplace While Keeping Your Soul Intact

Writers Club Press
an imprint of iUniverse.com, Inc.

For information address:
iUniverse.com, Inc.
620 North 48th Street, Suite 201
Lincoln, NE 68504-3467
www.iuniverse.com

ISBN: 0-595-12260-4

Printed in the United States of America

Contents

Exercises

ACKNOWLEDGEMENTS

I am extremely grateful to all my friends who encouraged me to put my knowledge and education in print. Though many say the experiences I lived through would make a great movie, I would hesitate to relive them again. Many friends who inspired my writing are: Louis Diaz, Marica Daley, Scilia Perez, Laural Llewellyn, Richard Bennett, Brian Hayes, Tom Ethans, Linda Allen and Richie Solomon.

This book would not have been written if not for the bullies and supervisors who attempted to torment my life and others. These individuals think they have won the fight only to find out they have created an educational tool which will prevent their activities from making more victims. To the Victor goes the spoils!

To my mother and father, Len and Nancy, who are proud of my accomplishments and encourage even more.

My two puppies who spent hours at my feet wondering why they weren't at a park playing in the grass.

And to God, for his mercy and grace, and for his always remaining with me. I was never alone in my tribulation. I know I am a child of God and pray for the poor souls who attack one.

INTRODUCTION

I began writing this book out of my own personal frustrations with the way companies view their working relationship with their employees. Times have changed in a large number of aspects, but many on top hold the idea that employees are disposable items. It is no wonder to me why so few employees are loyal to their employer. It is no wonder violence is the number one cause of death for women and the number two cause of death of men in the workplace.

Many of us spend hours attending college and schools to learn our trade and in hopes of landing the "job" that will make our career reality. What is missed by the educational system is the class on how to cope in the workplace and to handle finances. There are many tools we need to have to make us better employees. There are many traps for an unexpecting employee to be tangled in. We need to understand our frustrations and learn how to ventilate anger. Communication is key. More importantly is learning now not to be a target.

Do you speak up when a coworker or boss starts to bully you? How will your actions be interpreted if you remain silent on the issue? Whom should you talk to about your concerns? When should you start to worry about the security of your job? These are just a few of the questions this book will tackle. *Surviving The Workplace* is designed to give you the tools you need to have a more harmonious work environment.

Most battles do not come from outside forces, but rather from a battle within you. You see things differently than someone else. You may feel an injustice has occurred. If you did not feel this way, there would be no conflict.

We enter the workplace believing in fairy tales. There are many myths we continue to believe as we break into the workforce. Along the way, we begin to realize that to get ahead we must do something more. To stand our ground, we must make the right decisions. However, we can only make the best decision with the information we have. Not understanding your choices can lead to making the wrong one. Wrong choices can easily lead to disillusionment or even worse.

You may have already made some choices of which you are not proud. Do not worry, you have learned what not to do next time. Out of every decision you make, right or wrong, you can learn.

We also need to understand there are many situations that may be out of our control. That does not mean we are helpless. It means we do those things which will give us the best direction, the best opportunities, and most important the best outcome.

If you are experiencing problems in your current work environment, then you need to make sure you are making the right choices. You are gearing up to go to war. Yes, war. First you must defeat old ideas. Make sure you are going forward armed with useful information and thoughts.

You must practice. You will need to break old habits by changing the way you react to someone, or by letting something slide and not responding when you think you need to. Do not be hard on yourself if the first time you try something you perform the task at 50 % or less. That is why we practice.

Third, you will start to gather ground. Little by little you can take back what is ours and conquer what should be yours. Those individuals who target others are the ones needing special treatment, not you. If someone is harassing you or making you feel inadequate, the problem probably isn't you. As you learn how to fight back, you will gain back your self-confidence, and your pride.

The most important part of this book is to learn how to keep your soul intact while you battle evil. You are what is most important. If you lose a job or decide to move on, it will not really matter if you feel good about yourself. One job, one situation, does not make you who you are. It does not define your work ethic. Being the best person you can be does. What beliefs you chose to hold dear to your heart brings forth your character.

There are many employees who chose not to fight back and there are many that chose to bend their morals to keep a job, they are not the happy ones. These types of people do not feel good inside. They know they have lost some of their personal power to someone else. They also know that the next time a similar situation occurs it will be easier to look the other way or give up more of themselves until there is nothing left. You are the most powerful person you know.

I have designed this book with examples and information. There is no way I could cover every type of problem employees' face in the workplace. I hope that I have given you the tools to work through most of them.

Some of those tools will appear in my Boot Camp Training. At the end of each chapter, you will find an exercise. Practice is what makes us better. You will even find some of the exercises repeated. These are the most important tools you can take away from this book. I believe they bear repeating.

If your situation has become a hostile situation, I recommend you contact a legal professional. There is no reason an employee should put up with a hostile work environment. Beware that legal proceedings do take time. A good lawyer can help you with ideas for alternative suggestions to get immediate help. The same lawyer can help with responding to an accusation made toward you.

Always, in every situation, keep a journal or record of what is taking place. It may seem small now, but can escalate quickly into something much bigger.

So find a quiet place, bring a pen, and some paper—and let us get to work.

CHAPTER ONE

You're Not Alone!

There are many times in our life when we feel alone. When others back away from you, or do not want to admit what they see happening, it contributes to our feeling alone. Being harassed, bullied, or badgered at work by coworkers, supervisors, or any person on the job site can be a very lonely experience. Friends will tell you what you are going through is awful, but they do not really support you. Family, parents, siblings, and spouses may not believe you. They will tell you that you have become paranoid, or exaggerate the truth. Lawyers, human resources, other supervisors will tell you that you cannot fight it. You will even doubt yourself! You will question if you are person you are accused of being.

This book would not exist if companies across America saw their employees as a vital part of their company's growth and life. You are one of millions of Americans suffering at the workplace. It does not have to be that way.

The workplace landscape has changed drastically over the past decades. Where our father's father could find a job with a company and stay until their retirement has all but vanished.

Back in the 1940's and 50's loyalty was expressed by employees and to their company and by the company to their employees. A family type atmosphere existed. It wasn't that employees were treated as family members, but they were not seen as easily dispensable as they are today. Many more jobs were production line oriented and purely male dominated.

Wars came and created large changes in the makeup of the employees. Many men went off to fight, while women began to take up their positions in the work place. This shift of employees would forever change the work environment.

The late 60's and 70's a motto of "being anti-establishment" gave rise. Many young people viewed corporate America as the enemy. CEO's were literally seen as criminals. To take a job at a large corporate was to give in and loose the battle. Our parents were part of the establishment creating the greed the young people clearly rejected.

Our economy became stagnate. There was not a lot of growth or profit until the 80's. If you owned property or a business, your wealth grew. Buyouts became common place among businesses. Many hostile takeovers hit the news. Each time a company was bought out, employees would loose their jobs. Employees began to understand that their future was uncertain.

As companies grew in assets, others began to merge in order to complete with the big conglomerates. Employees found themselves out on the street three to four times in their career. Loyalty to the employee and to the company was destroyed.

Employees would abandon ship before they would be fired. When better opportunities arose, employees would take them.

The mergers continued through the 90's as companies tried to compete with each other in size and assets. Anti-discrimination laws attempted to regulate how a company chose its workers. Computers were introduced to corporate America, again changing the landscape forever. The work-at-home employee was born.

The American worker got lost in the hustle to make big money. Employees had no rights. You could be treated worse than your neighbor's dog. Bestowing dignity and honesty to the common employee was a sign of weakness. Male managers, who held the power in the hierarchy, sexually harassed female secretaries. The employee was helpless. The attitude was that if you did not like your place of employment, you could find another job.

Today there are still very few laws in place that protect the mental state of an employee. Though harassment laws have been passed they are hard to enforce and limited in their range of protection. Most often the employee who files such charges is the one who ends up being transferred into an inferior position or leaves the company. Harassment laws do not protect an employee from a boss who makes you their target because they simply do not like you. Nor to do they protect you if your boss is an alcoholic, or if the manager never learned how to play fair with the other children.

Very often we feel we are the only one who is putting up with inefficiency of a coworker, or correcting the mistakes of a supervisor without the proper avenues for solutions or the recognition we deserve. All too often we put up with being harassed, badgered or bullied by someone who has the "power" to do so. The results of such abuse are more than losing a job.

There are those of us who have chosen to fight. We have been winning.

Recently, I had lunch with a friend. Julie worked for a large aerospace company. She was one of 8,000 employees. Her division had over 500 employees and her department had 13. Julie had worked for this company for over 11 years. There had been no major changes. Suddenly she found herself fighting for her job and she could not believe it.

Julie's department supplied other departments with quotes and figures on various projects going on in the plant. Since these figures change almost daily, they were to be considered as guides and not actual representations of money spent. The cost analysis would take more time to allow all accounts to clear.

Julie told me that in recent months her boss had been piling projects on her left and right. She was doing the majority of the work in the office although there were several other associates working in her department. Julie never had time to sit around and have coffee for thirty minutes like her coworkers. In fact, she was putting in unauthorized overtime to get the job done. Julie began to keep a log of what assignments she and her colleagues were getting. Julie journaled everything.

The logs quickly revealed that she was carrying an enormous workload compared to the other employees within her department. She would have understood this if she was the most senior employee, but she was not. She had decided that she had to address the issue.

Attempting not to sound like she could no longer handle the disproportionate workload, she wrote a memo to her boss outlining her current list of projects assigned to her and how she was prioritizing them. This way she could let her boss know what her current workload was and set-up communication with her boss. The memo would serve a second purpose. The memo would record Julie's attempts to inform her boss of the working conditions she was facing just in case something down the road was to arise.

Six months later Julie was called into her boss' office. He began to ask her about work she had performed during this period. She was being accused of misquoting figure from a contract. Her boss demanded to know where she had acquired her information.

Since Julie had prepared the research four months prior, too far back to remember, Julie informed her boss she would go back and look through her files to see where she had obtained her information.

Less than a week later Julie was called back into her boss' office and presented with a letter concerning her inability to get the job done. This caught Julie off guard.

Julie was never given the opportunity to explain herself. Her extremely heavy workload was not taken into consideration. The fact that she had performed a myriad of different projects during this time period, plus maintained her daily workload without flaw or error was never mentioned.

Julie's journals, memos, and records paid off. She was able to prove her workload and current computer problems that hindered her work performance and her attempts to seek the right answers. You would think with all the evidence Julie presented that her boss would back off. However, things got progressively worse until Julie had no choice but to retained a lawyer. Then she was taken seriously.

There was never any need for any of the previous events to have taken place. Simply put, if her boss had only been able to communicate his needs and openly listen to Julie's concerns, none of the hostility created in this scenario would have occurred. The result of her boss's actions cost the company big.

Almost 50 % or the working population feels their job is stressful. More and more companies are asking employees to do more with less. Today's buzz words "reorganizing or restructuring" can boost stock prices and make stockholders happy, but strike fear into employees causing morale issues and often drop in productivity. It is bad enough coping with today's work place stress. It makes it harder when your coworkers are laid off on a weekly basis.

Many employees feel helpless in attempting to keep their position during a down-sizing. You are not helpless. There are several things you can do to reduce your chance of being downsized. As an employee, you can take additional classes in areas in which the company needs expertise. It is important to understand your company needs and make realistic solutions for problems. Always continue to have a positive attitude, take on extra responsibilities, and keep your door open. In other words, have the resume typed and let your friends (outside your company) know you are looking. You are not as fearful when you know there are other opportunities out there.

Most companies do not communicate well with their employees about what is taking place in the company structure. Nor do companies encourage employee involvement in decision making. By keeping employees well informed and encouraging their participation, companies can promote a more secure work force. Since this is not a high priority for the company, networking and making the right alliances can get you into the professional gossip circles. You will find more information on this topic in chapter twelve.

If layoffs are inevitable, your company should have an employee assistance program set up. Employee assistance programs teach employees about building good resumes, interviewing skills and more. Some may even teach other vocational skills to help employees get back on their feet. Many help with setting up interviews for laid-off employees. If your Company does not have a program like this in place, suggest it. Be careful on how you present any suggestion. It can backfire on you if not done in a positive and politically savvy method.

Steve worked for a mail delivery company on the west coast. He had seen bosses come and go over the years. He had worked his way up from a carrier and now works very close to the vice president of his company. During one summer, Steve was asked to help the vice-president pull off an affair he was having. Immediately, Steve thought having the "goods" on your boss meant you would be considered one of the good-old boys.

Steve's boss would spent many days at his "girlfriend's" house instead of being at work. Mike would messenger packages to him at her house so the vice president could get his office work done and appear as though he had been at work. Steve helped carry on this charade for a couple of months. Finally when the affair broke off, the vice president returned to his normal work schedule.

A few months later Steve's life became hell. The vice president started making accusations about Steve's work performance and lying about meetings between him and Steve, which never took place. The vice president said he had spoken to Steve on several previous occasions about his performance and Steve had not improved. In fact, Steve had not received any such verbal warnings.

Steve was asked to report to his company's human resources department. There he was given a written memo that his boss had prepared. This memo stated Steve had been verbally warned about several areas he needed to improve on and that Steve never did. Steve rebutted by stating his boss was trying to harass him into leaving by falsifying the facts. When asked by the human resources representative why this vice-president had it out for him, Steve revealed his story of the affair.

The only reason Steve is still employed at his company is the fact he had keep copies of everything he had did. Steve had the orders for the messengers, documentation on what was sent and to where. These documents included dates, times and addresses.

The very thing Steve thought would get him promoted almost cost him his job. Due to the information Steve had on his boss, his boss feared that Steve would reveal what he knew or could blackmail him with it so he had decided to get rid of Steve. Steve's misconception of how the "game" was played created a hostile work environment. Why Steve had decided to document and take the information home to a safe place, Steve only can explain as a hunch. Never before, at any other job, had Steve needed protect himself in this manner. The result of this incident wasn't all that Steve had hoped. In the process of saving his job, Steve was labeled as a troublemaker and has been unable to be promoted from his current position. Steve's image within the company has been damaged through no fault of his own.

Cindy's problem was quite different. She worked in a smaller office with two other ladies. Everyday Cindy would arrive at work early, prepare the coffee, and get her desk in order for the day's activities. Cindy had worked this way for a number of years.

She began to notice her other two associates were arriving late almost every day. As the year passed, the problem was irritating Cindy. It was now to the point that her associates would arrive 30 to 45 minutes late every day, had begun taking 2-hour lunches. To make up the time, one of the two workers would stay late and clock out both employees. The office manager knew what hours they were working because she had to sign all time cards daily. The two were not disciplined in anyway. It seemed as through the manager did not care.

The situation climaxed when one day Cindy needed to get off a little early for one of her children's school events. When she approached her office manager about coming in an hour earlier so she may leave an hour earlier, her office manager said no. This angered Cindy. In her mind, there was no difference between her coming in early and leaving early, and her associates were coming in late and making up the time at the end of the day.

Cindy knew she could not approach her manager on the subject since he was indifferent to the situation. Cindy attempted to discuss her problem with her director, but quickly found out no one wanted to do anything. Statements like "it's hard to prove what's going on," and "Your office manager can run her department however she sees fit," frustrated Cindy greatly. Cindy felt she was powerless to correct the situation.

Soon Cindy's work pattern began to change. Cindy no longer came to work early to get things ready. She no longer did extra tasks around the office like setting up birthday parties for coworkers or cleaning the community kitchen. Cindy started do such things as bringing work from home, like paying bills, to do on office time. Cindy's work productivity sank to an all time low, she produced only as much as her associates did and no more.

The company did suffer, however Cindy suffered more. She knew her work ethic was of a higher standard, but felt she was not being recognized for her efforts. She adjusted her pattern to match her office manager's attitude and the company's lack of concern.

There are many ways employees get back at a company when they feel they have been wronged. When denied a day off, employees call in sick. When denied a raise duly deserved, some steal company merchandise.

When not rewarded for hard work and diligence, work productivity falls. People naturally justify the scales when they perceive them to be skewed. Anybody who has worked for someone who is difficult wonders why the company does not see how these attitudes cost the company money. Even more troublesome to understand is why the company, once aware of the problem, does nothing to improve it. Remember the company is most concerned about turning a profit and making money for the shareholders. Trouble shooting is a cost which many employers do not see a return on.

Nowhere during your schooling did anyone tell you how to handle problems that occur in the workplace. We are told that if you work hard, you will get ahead. Yet, on a daily basis we see people who are promoted who bend all the rules. This work hard-get ahead fallacy is a cause for a lot of work-related frustration.

A typical conflict (lasting 5 days or less) in the workplace which involves three parties can cost a company over $50,000 in lost productivity, time, lower motivation, and health costs. $4.2 billion is lost each year by companies resulting from workplace violence. The economic result can be hidden in budgets and financial forecasts. The emotional cost cannot be totaled.

We need to understand the workplace. We need to explore the hidden prejudices. It is a requirement that we comprehend motives and desires. Having awareness of how your company complaint system works is vital. Every employee must fully understand both the obvious procedures and the undercurrent of the company. Any first level business major learns it is easy to find what a company thinks is important. One just needs to look at the company's overall financial report and see where the company spends the most money.

The same is true when examining a company's culture. Where the company spends its energy is what is important. Find out. Ask around. Your future could be directly tied to just how much you know as well as who you know.

Today's workplace is constantly evolving. What was once a steady, predictable income has become a climate breeding fear of a lost job and lost income. Down-sizing and re-engineering, buzz terms for the 90's, leave many employees wondering what they will be doing tomorrow. Where your father worked for a company his entire life, you now face the fact that you may have up to 7 different careers in your working life.

We cannot control many things. Understanding and knowing how to handle situations we can control, puts us on better ground. Eliminating undue stress is a natural result of becoming aware of your surroundings.

Boot camp training—Exercise one:

That's right, if you are reading this book you have joined the war against poor work environment. In fact, you are on your way to becoming the Work Place Super Hero.

Normally, I would not send a beginning swimmer to the deep end of the pool to learn how to swim, but this is serious information you need to have right at the start. It is your power of choice.

You are the most powerful person you know! Again, you are the most powerful person you know! Only you can decide what you are going to do, how you are going to do it, how you are going to react, and what choices you are going to make. No one, and I mean no one, can override your choices.

Your mission, better yet, assignment this following week is to chose one individual who deliberately tries to get under your skin with degrading remarks about you or your performance. It does not have to be a coworker. It can be a friend, family member, or anyone you choose. Say you choose Tom, a coworker who puts down your work at department meetings.

You will then choose a day—say a Tuesday—The day you have your department meeting. The night before place a note to yourself at your desk as a reminder that Tuesday will be different. You may want to code it like MOT (Tom backward). Also, the night before place a note on the back of your front door and on your steering wheel reminding yourself that you have chosen

Tuesday as the day Tom will not get the better of you. You will ignore his comments as if nothing were said.

If in the meeting Tom makes a comment you must address, ask a question. For example, if Tom says: "If Brad's report would have been done correctly my project would have been on time," play Blonde (as my girlfriends call it). "Tom, could you explain what was wrong with the report. Please." Tom will be expecting you to defend your report, and probably will not be able to come up with realistic concerns. If he does have some, you can address them immediately knowing exactly what to target.

That Person is: _____

I will: _____

CHAPTER TWO

Things They Never Taught You—Myths

As we grew up, we heard many things we believed to be true. As we grow older, we began to question some of those beliefs. You have started with Santa Claus or the Easter bunny. Although these two myths seem childish, a myth is still a myth.

There are many myths about the workplace. We grew up learning slogans about working hard, getting ahead, and taking risks. We enter the workplace with some unrealistic views. However, some of these views are given to us during the interviewing process.

I call it a "Courtship Deception." First, you hear about the job opening. Maybe you read an advertisement which promises equal opportunity, a great career, lots of advancements, and fantastic benefits. Then during the interview you are told what a great working environment their company has. You may even hear that the company is noted in a leading magazine as being one of the hundred top companies in the US for working moms, or workers' benefits, or community involvement.

It all sounds so lovely. You take the job. Within the first month, you find out that your manager will not adjust your schedule so you can pick up the kids. Maybe you find out from human resources that the benefits do not start for 120 days and you need them now. You become disillusioned. You are not the first employee this has happened to nor will you be the last. I have been on interviews where I was directly lied to about policies and about coworker pay scales with regard to my compensation.

Our courts have begun to notice how these deceptions harm employees. Managers can be held liable for gaining or maintaining your employment under false pretenses.

A myth many of us carry with us is that the work environment is more mature than your experience in high school. Don't be too sure. In fact you may have experienced less confrontations in high school than you do on your job. You may be experiencing a work environment that allows harassment or bullying. In that case, you are already questioning many things. Know that if you believe in yourself, you have already won. Everything directed at you is to diminish your self worth. Your attacker is spending countless hours and energy to think of new ways to tear you down. Wow, you must really be worth something.

As mentioned in chapter one, many of us were taught if you work hard, you will get ahead. Too many, that means if you sacrifice goofing off at the water cooler and stick to doing your job, your boss will notice. Your efforts will be rewarded when the next promotion becomes available. If you have been in the work force for any amount of time, you already learned this is not the case.

I am not saying hard work gets you nowhere, but do not rely solely on a saying.

Besides the saying "Work hard and get ahead," we have heard things like "Put your nose to the grind stone", "Pay your dues," and "Your ship will come in." If only those statements were 100 percent true, there would be no need to further your education, spend time at the water cooler, or sharpen your resume. All we would have to do is land a job, work hard and all our efforts would pay off. As we saw in chapter one, many obstacles appear within our lives which stop or slow down our forward motion. These obstacles appear from coworkers, family, economic climates, and unforeseen forces.

Your professional life is not detached from your home life. Quite often your work is how you identify yourself. Frequently the first question anyone asks you when you meet him or her is "What do you do for a living?" What we do and how we do it often reflects how we see ourselves. Let us flip that around because how we see ourselves is frequently intercedes on what we do and how we do it.

"Work hard and you'll get ahead." I would love to have a dollar each time I heard that saying while I was in school. No one told me upon entering the work force I would undergo more tests than high school, need to pass a fashion inspection, be judged on carrying a conversation or be graded on my career every six months. Nor was I ever told that no matter how hard I worked there is an unwritten law that your boss must find fault with you to justify not being paid the highest possible wage. Chapter Thirteen discusses how to handle negative information on your reviews. Just remember, never let negative information be placed in your personnel file without your comments. With all our education, we are not properly prepared to enter the workforce.

There are many successful people who have not completed higher education or who did not get a 4.0 or higher in high school. This fact alone tells you there is an error in thinking that good grades leads to high pay. Many times it is your view of money that keeps a person strapped from paycheck to paycheck. What I find even more interesting is that many accountants and CPA's also live from check to check. There are many strategies and books written on getting out of debt. Purchasing one or two of these books or attending a successful seminar is an extremely wise investment.

With financial freedom comes many other freedoms, such as not working for someone you can't stand.

Mike always tried to be the best employee possible. Perfection was a goal for him. After working for six months at a national travel agency, Mike had his first review. He received excellent marks in every category except for one. Mike decided he would concentrate on improving that area.

Upon working at the travel agency for one year, Mike received his next review and again received high marks in every category but one. The category had changed but the evaluation overall had come out to be the same.

When Mike went in for his third review, he received the identical results. At this point Mike had prepared himself to approach his manager regarding his reviews. He was told the company felt they had no employee had the ability to walk on water therefore, no one could receive a perfect review.

To be able to cope with the situation, Mike came up with a motto and plan he could control. If his company was going to find something wrong with him anyway, he should be the one to choose. Mike picked a category on his review, which the company did not care too much about and eased up on trying to meet the company's goals. Mike then put his energies into meeting and surpassing those goals that the company would recognize.

What Mike had realized is the outcome of his reviews could not be improved beyond his current standing. He did have the control to make a change. Mike knew could ability to control his frame of mind. In addition, Mike wanted to spend his energy where he could excel. Mike allowed himself to ease up in a nonessential area. His motto" If they are going to knock me down on my skills, I will give them something to knock down." Holding this attitude helped Mike be more in control of the situation.

"Pay your dues" was the saying Chris had heard when she first entered the workforce. Originally, she thought she should not expect anything special until she had put in some time. Years passed. Every time Chris would approach her boss on the topic of being promoted Chris kept hearing the same saying. She heard it from bosses, Coworkers and executives while she watched younger men go right up the ladder. Chris had more education and more work experience, yet she was suppose to be paying her dues. It did not take Chris long to figure out that paying dues was only a statement of suppression.

Never stall at going after what you want. No matter what is said to you, go after it. Age, sex, education are not barriers. They can actually be assets.

Many believe the cost of taking on a company against harassment, badgering or being "bullied" is too high.

You must take responsibility for you and where you are. If you are employed, then you interviewed for your job and you accepted the position at the wage you were offered. No one made you take that particular job, working for that particular company. No one makes you get up in the morning and go in to work.

It is very important that you accept some responsibility. If you accept none, then stop reading this book. There is nothing more you can do. Everything is out of your control. If you acknowledge the fact that you have some responsibility in your current situation, then you have the power to do something about it.

Attend seminars that either improve your current work or are in an area which you are interested. Go back to school and acquire a degree or take some classes to brush up on current trends. Purchase some books on fantastic resumes and resume letters. Talk to friends about how they like their work location and job and ask them what is out there. Let people within your current company know want to move up or into a new department. Find out who within your organization is responsible for hiring individuals in the department in which you are interested. Set up a number of informational interviews. The bottom line is taking action.

Doing something, anything, will help relieve any feeling you may have about feeling trapped. You will know you are in the process of improving yourself and your work situation. In the process of gaining knowledge or attending classes, you may meet someone who is looking for your qualifications who respects the fact you are doing something about your current situation.

The possibilities are limitless. You are not stuck working for someone who does not recognize you for your efforts or abuses your talents. You know you are just passing the days away until you reach your goal and move up and out of your current position.

We should have been taught such sayings as "keep growing," "Never feel powerless," and "there is always something you can do." These statements give you personal power. They put you in control. Remember you have always been in control.

"Stress is the same everywhere and at every job, so why change." This is a myth I heard hundred of times at my job site. Not only is that statement false, there are many other statements which we carry around believing to be true. Most stress comes from lack of planning. Plan your job responsibilities. Know what deadlines you have and how long different projects take. Set priorities, work on easy solutions first and the more complicated ones next. Planning relieves stress.

Stress is not the same for everyone. It is how you respond to a situation that adds to your stress. If you feel you are not a good public speaker and you have been asked to do a presentation, you may feel extremely stressed. However, if you are good at budgeting and are given a budgeting assignment, you just get it done. There are people who love to speak who do not get stressed at presentations, but may get stressed if handed a budgeting assignment. Find those items or situations in your job which give you stress and try to eliminate them. If public speaking is a fear of yours, take a class or join a public speaking club, like Toastmasters, and learn.

Stress, in and of itself, can be good for you. Mismanaged stress can cause physical and emotional problems. Stress can even kill you. Make sure you are managing those items and situations that are in your control. Prioritize, take time out, and give yourself reminders (e.g., notes and pictures). These are all techniques to reducing stress. I use to keep a picture of a beagle in a full run on my office wall. Managers thought I loved beagles. However, that was not what it meant to me. When I was going through some sharp harassment from a boss, when a friend told me "Hey, they don't kick dead dogs. You must be doing something right."

Just because there is no outright sight of stress doesn't mean you are stress-free either. Medications or alcohol can mask symptoms. Sleepless nights or short tempers may be signs that are overlooked.

My favorite myth of all time is "Life is not fair." Have you noticed what person utters that phrase most often? The answer is the incompetent supervisors who have no other way to explain their poor judgment, lack or experience or stupid decision. Life, itself, is pretty fair on the whole. Adding the human element has made it most unfair.

Your are worth the price you give yourself. No one you will ever meet will raise that price. Only you can.

Boot camp training—Exercise two: Get out the paper and pen.

If you believe you are being harassed, start a journal. It is best to get the type of journal that either has dates already or one you can date where the pages are in book form. It gives you a better legal edge when pages cannot be moved around. There are many journal products on the market.

Make sure to document things that are said to you, looks or physical actions directed at you. If there are others present at the time these actions occur, note their names and positions within the company. The more information you have, the better you will fare.

Keep copies of items that support your claims. Managers have even put their harassment in memos and e-mail form. Nothing like having it in writing. Be careful that you do not take home items that are considered company assets. A Company can come after you legally for stealing from them.

Check off when completed:

☐ Purchase a journal
☐ Find a favorite writing pen
☐ Start writing.

CHAPTER THREE

How To Handle Your Boss.

Sometime during your career, you will run into someone whose sole purpose in life is to make yours miserable. At least it will seem like it. The workplace is not immune.

We must tackle some basic issues first. Good communication is important. Though a good manager should already understand this concept, you may be the one required to establish communication channels. Use friendly conversation to build a relationship of mutual trust and respect. Make sure what is expected from others is clearly established. If there are any vague procedures, ask questions. Keep a professional attitude while maintaining a confident relationship. Strive for a happy medium between being too friendly and appearing cold and distant.

Sometime in your working career, you will have a disagreement with a supervisor. How you handle that disagreement can influence you next career move. Time is a tool you should use.

If your supervisor presents a problem to you, take in the information. Do not react immediately. If it is a criticism about your work performance and you feel under attack or angry, simply tell your supervisor you would like some time to think about it before responding.

Take some time to think before you react. This gives you time to gather your thoughts and to be better prepared with a response. Write down those things that come to mind and prepare the issues you feel are important to this matter. Make sure any issues or points you bring forward you can back up with fact. If you have someone you can talk with about this situation (a spouse or friend in another company), have them look at your response. Make sure it is clear of any personal attacks or unfounded statements.

Do not let a lot of time pass, your supervisor may feel you are stalling. As soon as you are ready, make an appointment with your supervisor to sit down and discuss your point of view. There are mainly four outcomes from this approach. One, your supervisor sees your point of view and agrees with you. Second, your supervisor still disagrees and you are at deadlock. You may have to go higher for a resolution or bring in a third party to arbitrate. Three, a compromise is reached where each give in a little. Fourth, the conflict escalates. This is most likely to occur when at least one of the parties involved is not professional and lacks reasoning skills. Supervisors who like to harass or bully have never needed to sharpen those skills. It is unfortunate that many companies in America stand behind their supervisor's decision or attitude, right or wrong, at the cost of a good employee.

Conflict should not be seen as only being destructive, but as constructive. Conflict is a normal function in any group setting or organization. It allows ideas. We choose whether conflict will strengthen us or weaken us.

Make sure you know your company's policy and procedure for grievances. Check your employee handbook. If nothing is there, ask your human resources department for a copy of the policy. If there is nothing in writing—you can ask for it. Remember if your company has not had the forethought to have a policy, be careful. Companies sometimes do not put policies in writing so they do not have to abide by their own rules.

When in meetings, take notes. Many instructions are given at meetings, only later to be dismissed. Notes are a good way to defend your position. When a supervisor asks why you prepared a report in a certain fashion and you can tell them that "in the August 27th meeting you stated…," you're covered.

As employees, we need to understand the concept that most people do not like any situation which they have no control over. Many frustrations between employees and their bosses begin with the fact they feel as though they are powerless to do anything except complain to coworkers about their particular situation.

Attempting to understand your boss' motivation for his/her attitude gives the employee a perspective to consider. Motivational factors can be as simple as needing to point the finger at someone else to save their skin, or as complicated as the boss viewing you and your work ethic as a threat to their job.

Mary had a boss who loved to scream and yell. It seemed as if he needed to intimidate one person a day or he was not satisfied. A perfect example was one day when Mary heard her boss yell from his office "Who out there wants to come in and get yelled at?" Mary thought he was joking. She entered his office and asked what she could do for him. He just began yelling about some problem Mary had nothing to do with. Mary was drove to tears. "Why would anyone want to do this?" she asked.

Mary could not understand the motivation behind her boss' actions. Pulling out a sturdy chair, I had Mary climb on top and stand there. That simple action made Mary embarrassed. Then I asked her to stick her arm straight out and point. Next was the hardest part for Mary. I told her to yell as loud as she could and to blame someone for something. Yes, actually yell: "Why did you do that. You've messed everything up. You're an idiot!"

Mary's first attempt was weak. I instructed her to do it again. Yell! Point! Mary tried again. This time she was louder with more emotion behind it. After about five attempts, she got the idea. Mary became her boss. The anger behind her words began to be heard.

Quietly I asked her how she felt. She thought for a moment and replied "All powerful." I asked her again, to dig deeper. Mary thought a little harder and said, "I feel tall." Mary started to drop her arm and I immediately told her to put it back. She complained "I'm tired." Suddenly a realization hit her. In her excitement she realized how much energy her boss was spending trying to keep up this "all-powerful" image of his.

Upon stepping down from the chair, Mary felt how her boss feels when he is not up, being tall. Mary was surprised.

I asked Mary to do one more thing for me. "The next time your boss starts yelling at you, turn your back to him. If you are sitting down, standup and turn. Do not face him. The simple action of turning your body away removes power."

One of the first lessons you would learn as a karate student is if you face forward to your enemy, you are totally exposed. The normal karate-fighting stance is with one foot back and your body slightly turned with arms bent and up. This stance limits the access to your body making you a much harder target to hit, keeping vital areas away from the attacker. This same principle applies here.

There are laws that do not allow for a hostile work environment. The best way to be able to present such a case either to your internal human resources department or outside counsel is to maintain a journal. I would recommend a diary type journal that has month/date/time. Make sure the journal pages cannot be removed or changed. The pages should be bound in a book type journal. The reason behind this requirement is because the journal is more tamperproof and you cannot be accused of changing information. For your own protection, it will keep everything in order and since pages are not removable, so they are not easy to loose. Do not keep your journal at work.

Any information, documentation or anything else you need to present your case should be kept in a safe place away from the people you plan to use it against.

Journaling what happened, who was present, and when it happened is essential. Showing a pattern over time is paramount. If certain situations warrant the immediate attention of human resources or a higher manager, do not hesitate to present your problem. Make sure you are not emotional at the time you present your information.

Do not stop journaling. Note whom you reported the incident to, what was said, and what the outcome was. Make sure you note any possible retaliation which may occur due to your report.

Dan was the type of worker who spotted errors in many of the documents that passed through his desk. Often he may stumble across information that could cause his company problems regarding their product. Dan always took the time to report the information to his supervisor backing it up with the proof he found.

It did not take Dan long to realize his supervisor was taking all the credit. Most employees recognize that speaking to your supervisor's boss is a sure way to get you into hot water with your supervisor. How could Dan let executives know he was the one who made the discoveries?

This is where a computer can become a good friend. Most companies now have a network within their company. This network allows individuals to e-mail one another in a less formal setting. If you do not have e-mail access, memos will still do the same. Dan began to e-mail his supervisor while sending copies to the upper management of his division. He structured the e-mails in such a way they were not threatening to his supervisor. Dan's approach was to state that he wanted to make sure everyone was in the loop here and he would go on to explain what he had found. He then ended his e-mails with the phrase similar to "if anyone has further information regarding what I have found, I would appreciate it if you would contact me." This technique allowed Dan's supervisor and manager to see the work Dan was performing while seeming to be asking for advice.

Some of the most important advice any employee should remember is never let a bad situation get the best of you. If you are written up, wait a couple of days. Then take the time to write a rebuttal. Review it before you hand it in. Look to make sure you are not being accusatory. Have all your facts straight and in order. Make sure what you are saying is easily understood and clear. If you have back up, copy it and submit it with the rebuttal. Remember, state information which relates to the problem. Do not bring in external information or additional problems unless they are relevant to the problem at hand.

Your precise, professional presentation of the facts presents an image of you. It is very possible the situation you see as a problem can open doors. That's right. Sherry was in this identical situation. She had been written up for something that she wasn't even involved in.

Sherry had always kept a journal of things going on around the office. She journaled every assignment given to her. She kept copies of documents that could potentially present a problem. After being written up, Sherry began to gather all her documentation. She reviewed it. In doing so she realized she had a great case against her director.

She spent about one week preparing her rebuttal to the accusations made against her. The rebuttal looked like a well-prepared report. She addressed the rebuttal to her director, but copied the vice president, human resources, and asked for a copy to be placed in her file.

When the vice president received his copy, he was impressed, very impressed. Approximately one month later a large project was handed to the vice president. He remembers the quality and professional presentation of Sherry's rebuttal. Sherry was promoted and asked to take the assignment on.

Many times it is hard for us to understand how something good can come out of an unfavorable circumstance, but it can. If you allow yourself the time to step back for a few minutes and study the situation, you may realize how you can take almost any set of circumstances and use them in your favor.

When we take the time to understand the motivation behind our boss' attitude, we begin not taking their actions personal. We realize the problem is theirs. We comprehend how much energy this individual is expending to maintain their hostile attitude. You actually begin to feel sorry for them. You may even catch yourself laughing at a situation you could never laugh at before. You are no longer the target or the victim.

You now know what steps you need to take, how to approach a situation, and that you have a responsibility to improve your career growth by learning from each experience. Of course, it is always nicer when you are able to approach you manager and openly discuss what you are feeling or how you perceived and attitude or situation to be. That type of relationship is ideal. I would always recommend open communication as the best approach to clearing the air. I realize that quite often this is not possible.

Be creative in your thinking. Getting through a front door can be almost impossible at times. Look for a back door or another way to approach the situation. It can be a challenge to come up with another avenue.

If you have a friend whose work ethic you admire and are in a position equivalent or higher than your bosses, preferably at a different company, speak to them. Get their insight.

Remember you do not have to approach the situation immediately in most cases. Gather your thoughts, make sure your feelings are intact, and get as much information as you can. Choose your battles wisely. It is not necessary to fight every comment or problem that comes your way. Evaluate what has taken place and if it's harmful to your career. Fighting every little thing that comes your way will brand you as a troublemaker. Then when a "real" problem comes along, you will probably be ignored. Do not be a passive-Annie.

There are battles that need to bes fought. Sometimes a supervisor could be testing you. Think it through before taking action. Make sure you are not being chiseled at either. Harassment can start out with little things and quickly grow into overwhelming conditions. If you feel uneasy about a situation or feel you are a target, do not take it lightly. You are probably correct.

In addition, remember never to embarrass someone more powerful or in a position of power. Make sure not to sabotage your own career. Do not let jealousy or your ego be your motivation. Drugs and alcohol are destroyers of many people's career. It is important to always be seen as a team player.

The one regret most employees have is that they did not confront the person who was harassing or targeting them. They did not get their dignity back and now feel they have comprised their self-respect. Too many of these compromises promotes a feeling that we have no right to fight.

In addition to having problems with a manager or supervisor there have been reported cases where managers have lied to string a worker along. In *Forbes* October 1999 magazine there is an article that talks about a ruling on the side of an employee that has become a landmark case. A company was downsizing and a manager had been strung along to think he had been doing a fine job and that his position with the company was secure. The trouble began in November of 1987 when 17 of his employees were let go. Fearing for his job the manager asked his boss about the situation and was reassured that this loss would not affect him. In 1989, some two years later, his job was reclassified, however he was not informed. He didn't learn about the downgrade until August 1992. The manager was fired for a sexual harassment charge seven months later.

Unable to find work the ex-manager sued for $9.2 million in lost earnings due to the fact his boss had lied to him. He won $24.6 million (which was the amount after the trial judge reduced the jury's verdict).

Employers are duty-bound not to deliberately deceive their employees. This is not unlike laws already in place when you hide a defect in a house you are selling or a car you are buying. We must wait to see if the Miller vs. Mackenzie case will survive any appeals.

Boot camp training—Exercise three: It is time to take your medicine.

Your assignment this week is to rent or see a comedy movie. Make sure it is one you enjoy. It is even better if it is a comedy you enjoyed a few years ago during less stressful times. Not only will the comedy make you laugh, you will remember good things about the past.

I like to have mini marathons when I need a lift. I might rent three Harrison Ford or Val Kilmer movies or an evening of strong leading ladies (like Jodie Foster). You may want to rent two or three comedies or uplifting films—get you favorite snacks and drinks and sit back and enjoy.

The idea here is to have fun. Laughter is the best medicine. It has been medically proven that laughter releases certain chemicals in the body making us feel better.

Make it a point to remember certain lines from you favorite films that make you smile. I loved the movie Princess Bride. In the movie Cary Elwes plays a farm boy turned pirate. He attempts to save his lady from a prince who wants her as his bride, but she loves the farm boy. At one point in the film Cary's character is dead, in fact he was almost dead all day (you have to see the film for that one). He and his friends are storming the castle—sort of—to retrieve his true love. The farm boy/pirate has been unable to move any body parts all day. He moves his head. His trusted friend sees him move and gets emotionally encouraged. Cary's character looks at his friend with curiosity and says "And a little head jiggle makes you happy."

When I see a coworker getting rave reviews for work not worth its weight of the paper it's written on you will hear me quote that line. I have given that line a double meaning (I'm sure you can guess). it makes me laugh. Most important is that no one else understands what I am saying. It is much better than saying something I may regret or taking the matter too seriously.

Find a favorite line that triggers a positive response in your attitude and try it out.

Movies to Rent: _____

Lines I Love: _____

CHAPTER FOUR

How To Handle The Coworker

Any person who has been in the work environment knows trouble does not always come from the top. Coworkers have their own agenda. Some want to discredit your work, others are waiting for one error they can place on the front page of a newspaper. There are many obstacles waiting for each one of us. If you can recognize which ones you need to be concerned about, you will find a number of them fall to the wayside.

Colleen's work environment was a very hectic one. She assisted a real estate manager by maintaining certain facilities. The office she worked at had approximately 15 people in it. The only person with a full office was her boss.

Colleen had been unaware of the animosity her coworkers held. The manager had brought in Colleen when the assistant job opened. Having worked for her boss at a previous real estate office, she jumped at the chance to work with him again. Several other office personnel felt they should have been promoted. A game begun to discredit Colleen.

28

What started to happen to Colleen was the stuff of which soap operas are made. Coworkers would take paperwork off her desk and throw it in the trash when she would leave for lunch. Upon returning Colleen would think she had misplaced her work and spend wasted time trying to locate the paperwork. It didn't take long for her to figure out it wasn't her. Working late one night copying a large document, she noticed something in the recycle bin. It was her work. Work, that earlier in the day, had became lost.

Colleen begun to remove all documents from her desk anytime she left the office. She double-checked her work to make sure nothing else was changed or altered. She even grew suspicious when she would have to leave to use the ladies room. Working under these conditions became unbearable.

Colleen approached her boss with the information. She did not know who was doing it and she did not care. However, Colleen needed a solution. Her boss came up with one. He had a small office built and gave it to Colleen. It did not resolve the underlying problem, but did give Colleen piece of mind.

Whenever there is a problem which does not allow you to perform your work, communicate. Communication is very important. How you communicate is just as important. Knowing who is the right person to speak with (chain of command) is as important as how you approach the topic. If you are aware of what a coworker maybe doing, speak to them. Try to figure out their motivation. Remember: If a coworker, or any person, is attempting to put you down, destroy your work ethic, or sabotage you, the problem lies with the attacker. You are fine. In fact, there is a good chance you are too good. Did you ever think your attacker is insecure about their own work performance and you are making them look bad?

Take a hard look around before you approach any situation. One quick lesson any emergency technician learns is to stop and evaluate an emergency scene before entering it. Look for fallen electrical wires, smell to see if there may be gas, and survey the entire sight because what may look obvious as the culprit that caused the situation might not be it at all. Use this principle here.

Maria worked in a department store maintaining inventory levels in the women's apparel department. She had done her job well for the past 3 years. Suddenly her boss began questioning everything she did. Maria became paranoid every time she completed a report. She constantly had to prove what she did and why she did it.

As Maria would explain her work, her boss accidentally let it slip that a coworker was bringing these questions to her attention. Maria did not understand why a coworker would have the right or the time to question her work. It was not the coworker's responsibility to do so. Maria became angry.

Immediately Maria wanted to confront the coworker, but decided to talk to an old friend first. Maria knew that speaking to someone she felt confident with and who she admired as a manager, she would feel more confident when she made her decision on how to handle the situation. Maria's friend brought forward something Maria never thought of—her boss was allowing the action. To complicate the situation, it was apparent Maria's boss did not know the answers to the questions being posed by her coworker or she would not have to ask Maria.

Her friend pointed out that Maria could speak with her boss, however due to Maria's situation she was powerless to enact change. If the problem could not be resolved through conversation, Maria would have to go to her human resources or labor relations person to get help. The advice helped Maria a great deal. She had never thought about her boss' involvement in her problem.

Companies are slowly growing more aware of every employee's needs. Federal guidelines have help create channels of communication to report work ethic violations, harassment and other employee concerns with confidentially. If your company has a channel in place, do not be afraid to use it. Sometimes using an anonymous letter or memo is the only solution you may have.

Always explore your avenues. Make sure you are not reacting to a situation, but taking the appropriate action. Approaching the individual 'causing' the problems can solve most of them. Many of the statements made that we instantly take as directed to us are poorly made. For instance, in a recent company where several promotions were recognized, an executive stood up in front of everyone and proclaimed "We have taken the best people and promoted them. Our company is going to be the best." Sounds good, until you think about it. What if you were not promoted—are you chopped liver? Do not automatically jump to the conclusion that is what they meant. Chalk it up to poor English skills and narrow thinking.

Maybe your approach to a coworker could be causing the problem. If you found an error in a coworker's performance, how do you present it? Personally I like to make sure I am 100% right. I always ask the coworker "I don't understand how you arrived at this number. Can you help me?" Many times, as we go back through the work the coworker finds the error. Amazing enough, sometimes they show me where I was wrong. Both of us come out ahead. This is a non-accusatory approach.

When starting a new job we all want to make new friends. It would be better to be friendly and to form friendships after you get to know the players. On your first day, make sure you introduce yourself to everyone. Do not get caught up in making sure you are in a click or group. You are the new kid on the block and that makes you a very good target. If there are feuds within a department, employees will try to gain your alliance immediately. Do not be fooled.

Get to know which individuals are the movers and the shakers. Make friends with the ones who are serious about their careers and have the most potential to move up.

Make sure the right people see you. Deliver memos yourself. Stay out of harms way of those individuals who are trouble-makers.

Keep communication channels open with your boss. Your approach can easily determine the outcome of a conversation. Communication can be a scary adventure if you have never traveled down that road. Do not jump in all at once. Try little items, anything. Be creative in your approach. You can even make a game of it.

Tell a few people the same thing and see how their reactions vary. I am sure you have noticed that two different people can tell you the same thing but you react totally different. Could it be who told you, how they told you, or what they said that made the difference? It could be one or a combination of any of these factors. You decide how to interrupt the communication and so does your listener.

Always watch your back. You could be surprised why a coworker would want to attack you. It could be as silly as a smile from the UPS delivery person to jealously about your work ethic. Without fuel for a fire, it is hard to get it to burn.

Nevertheless, remember to give your coworkers the benefit of the doubt when situations arise. Whenever possible avoid taking sides in work place confrontations. Make up your own mind regarding company issues.

Stay out of the rumor mill. Do not spread gossip. Do not become someone who tears down alliances. Rumors are harmful to both those who spread them and those who listen. If you are unsure about something that is said to you by a coworker and the information is important to you, go to the source. Ask if what you have heard is true or not. Do not let false ideas or fears gain mental ground. When there is good communication in a company rumors cannot be spread as easy.

Praise you coworkers. Let them know when you think they have done a good job. People like to be praised and respected. Give credit where credit is due. Both of these concepts build goodwill.

Think before we act and speak, but speak up.

Boot camp training—Exercise four: Taking responsibility

It is important that you take responsibility for the situation in which you may find yourself. I am not saying the whole situation is your responsibility, only a portion. Even taking a low percentage, say 2% is a very necessary step.

Why would this be so important? Because if you have no responsibility regarding the situation you find yourself in a situation that becomes hopeless there is nothing you can do about it. You would be powerless to help yourself.

Since you have stayed in the situation (not found another job) or have not spoken up, then you have let the situation continue and are partly responsible. Owning up to—let's say 2% of the problem—gives you the world. Now you can act, you have some control.

❑ You have already started journaling and recording what is taking place.

❑ You are attempting to react differently to statements or harassment aimed at you.

❑ You have laughter as your medicine against taking things too seriously. You are getting ready to step up to the plate.

Repeat this line three times: I am taking a two-percent responsibility for the situation I currently find myself.

Now write what that responsibility is. It could be that you have let statements made to you get the better of you or you haven't keep good records to be able to present your situation to someone in the company who could respond and resolve the conflict.

My responsibility is: _____

_____

I will now take action by: _____

CHAPTER FIVE

Motivators And Attitudes

To better understand the work environment, one needs to better understand human nature. Since the beginning of human civilization, psychologist, sociologists, scientist, and many others have pondered human attitudes and behaviors, as well as what motivates an individual. We could call this chapter Psychology 101. In this chapter many theories are presented in a short overview. Throughout this book you will see how employees attempt to solve work place problems by applying these theories.

One could go back as far as the late 19th century when motivational theories were influenced by psychologist Sigmund Freud, and functionalist William James. Freud's theories viewed human behavior as being motivated by two biological instincts, life and death. While James' theory dealt with tapping into instincts such as fear, cleanliness and love, we can hold a perspective that the survival side of the human equation creates motivation. However, since both of these theories are only labeling motivations they cannot be subject to empirical testing.

Clark Hull incorporated into his theory a mathematical equation of B =D x I x H, or that behavior is a result of three factors: 1) drive, 2) incentive and 3) habit. From my own past experiences in the work force, this type of theory seems to make more tangible sense to me.

Many of us have heard of Maslow's hierarchy of needs theory. Maslow held the view that human behavior is a purely biological need for survival. Human needs were ranked and one need had to be fulfilled before moving to fulfill another. The most basic need was hunger and thirst or basic needs. Going up the pyramid would be safety, followed by belonging and love, then self-esteem, and finally self-actualization. However, many researchers oppose Maslow's theory and believe that a pattern exists, not the shape of a pyramid but rather based on a social and economical pecking order.

Hertzberg expanded Maslow's theory by adding more motivating factors. Like Maslow, Hertzberg's theory is based more on internal factors such as hunger and security, rather than external factors such as incentives.

Hertzberg's theory is known as the Motivation-Hygiene theory. His research drew him to the conclusion that there are two levels of motivational factors; Dissatisfiers and Satisfiers. Disatisifiers are those areas or factors which need to meet a level of satisfaction. Such factors are job security, salary level, working conditions, company policies and fringe benefits. Satisfiers, on the other hand, build motivation. These factors are achievement, recognition, responsibility, and advancement.

Around World War Two, theorists began to expand their way of thinking and added such ideas as personal belief being an additional motivator. The Cognitive Theory relied on the basis that behavior is a function of a person's beliefs and expectations. People will make decisions about their behavior patterns based on what they believe will occur.

From this theory the control theory was born. Howard Klein's model of the control theory presents implications of viewing goals and feedback as a two-part process. One such grounded theory is goal setting. The basic framework for this theory was developed by Edwin Locke and is used by a growing number of managers.

From there a number of theories or management styles have been created. Content theories can use goal setting by involving the needs of the employee. Process Theory works directly with what the employee believes the outcome to be. The Reinforcement theory uses goal setting as the foundation for use for reinforcement. Management by Objectives is also associated with goals and is sweeping the nation.

What management seems to overlook is what happens when an employee perceives a discrepancy between the amount of work being performed to the amount of rewards received, motivation is reduced. The Equity Theory, developed by J. Stacey Adams, et. al, expands this idea by stating when an employee feels a discrepancy occurs, an employee is left with few choices. An employee can either get the outcome increased, such as pay, or decrease their input by doing less work.

Why discuss all these motivation theories? These discussions are to get you to think on other levels. These theories do not apply only to management to incorporate in an emploe's review, you as an employee can use them, too. Each theory holds a piece or truth to it. Each of us has factors that motivate us. Do you know your supervisor or coworker well enough to understand where their behavior pattern is coming from?

Remember, as an employee any idea which you may have that can help your company may and should be proposed by you. If your company lacks programs that encourage motivation, propose one.

B.F. Skinner brought forward the ideas of reinforcement and operant conditioning. In other words the power of reward and punishment. Using this theory, when an employee performs to the level of work desired by the organization, then a reward should match the behavior. This reward should be closely connected to the behavior. Time intervals play a large role here.

Can an employee to a supervisor use this theory? Sure it can. Remember that the reinforcement must be of value to the person receiving it. You cannot assume one reward is good for all. Be creative.

This is where you become the detective. Try to understand the behavior you are observing. Is the person insecure? Have they had experiences in the past creating the wall you now see? Are they taking advantage of someone else because they can?

Also, examine is their actions are truly effecting your job performance. Are you upset because you feel the person in question is getting more rewards than you? Are you being unjustly treated?

I cannot say it enough times, think before you jump. Look at the situation from as many angles as you can. Decide if you need to stand up for yourself. Pick your fights wisely.

It is important to stand up for yourself when it is appropriate. Do not become the type of individual who holds in your anger or fears.

Boot camp training—Exercise five: Let's go shopping.

Have you ever been out shopping when you came across that item you just had to have? Did you look at the price? Did it matter? Remember you bought it anyway? What happened after you got home? Did you have buyer's remorse?

A number of years ago I bought a painting from a new upcoming artist for much more money than I should have been spending. When I saw the picture it made me feel free and feminine. I just knew I had to have it. When I got it home I smiled as I unwrapped it for it's packaging. I really should have paid a bill or two. I just had to have this picture.

Today I have the picture proudly displayed in my entry hall. It is the first thing visitors see when they come over. I now own three other works by this same artist. I learned that day that I was worth more than the painting. Every time I look at the piece of art on my wall I remember what I am worth.

Find something that you bought that makes you feel good. If you have not purchased anything, start looking. Take that special item and place it where you can see it everyday. Stare at it when you feel like it. You can't help but smile. No one else needs to know what that item means to you. If you do have some one to share it, it's even better.

My item is: _____

It makes me feel: _____

CHAPTER SIX

Education And Experience

Have you thought about getting more education or a different career experience? Why would this be a chapter in a book about surviving the workplace? Because the more leverage you have, the better off you will be and feel.

You do not need to get another degree necessarily. You can attend seminars on topics available to you from work, or take some adult night school course, which generally run 1 to 6 weeks long, and are a minimal cost to you.

If you haven't finished a degree you started, maybe now is the time. It is proven that individuals with degrees generally make substantially more than those who don't. Workers with 4 year degrees earn 73% more than those without a four-year degree. In 1994, individuals who are college graduates had a lower unemployment rate (1.8 %) compared to those who did not graduate from high school (14.3%). The average earnings for a master degree graduate is over $47,000, a bachelor's degree over $36,000, an associate degree over $27,000 and a high school degree just over $21,000.

Look into reimbursement from your company. Many companies today offer paid tuition, either full or partial, for taking college courses. This does two wonderful things for you. One, you get further education making you more valuable to the company and two, taking classes makes the company aware you are taking the initiative to improve without tooting your own horn. Companies that invest in their employees want to reap the benefits of that investment.

You, on the other hand, now have more for your resume. You are actively showing you can learn new things, and you believe in improving your knowledge. Companies are always looking for people with positive attitudes. I call it a "Can-do Attitude." Just put yourself in the place of a manager hiring someone. Whom would you pick? Someone who has an "I know it all attitude" or someone who is willing to do what it takes and can do anything you need them to do? Would you like to hire someone who is willing to learn new things or someone who is willing to try new challenges? On the other hand, would you rather have someone who cannot change?

If you think learning a new idea is not needed—let's think about new words and ideas that have cropped into our vocabulary in the last decade. Terms like e-mail, Internet, search engines, and on-line were not used. Words like mouse, surfing and windows all have new meanings. If you have not become part of the New World of technology—where are you? Hopefully you are getting ready to retire.

What about changing careers? Many people find that the career they started out in is not exactly what they were looking for or that another area or career within their field would suit them better. Life changes bring new ideas, new life requirements, and ways of thinking. You can't just go out a get a new career.

Look at your current employer. See if you can make a change within the company where you now work. Talk to the head of the department in which you want to work. If that is not possible, see if there are avenues within your company to gain experience for your new career. A good example is the fact you would like to work in human resources instead of your current position. If your company is having a school day for children to come and find out about careers at your company. Check to see if your alma mater is coming. If they have not been invited, see if you can invite them and arrange for them to attend. Be a greeter when your school arrives and even offer to speak to the students about your current job and how you got there. Get involved.

In your cover letter to new prospective employers you will make reference to all these activities. You can state, "I have attended seminars (list seminars) and was active in my employer's school-to-career workshops for students of local community schools in preparation to obtain a position in this career field."

Understanding your personal finances is necessary. What does this have to do with your career? You ask. It's really Simple. If you find yourself living from paycheck to paycheck, you are creating more stress than you need. Changing the way you think about money can change you entire life. Creating opportunities for investment and self-reliance relieves you of having to depend on a company's well being for your survival. Take courses recommended by financially successful people you know, and read books.

Knowing you have healthy alternatives sets your mind at ease. You will be less stressed when you hear rumors about layoffs, or if your supervisor starts harassing you.

Boot camp training—Exercise six: Let's work off that stress.

What hobby or sport or activity do you enjoy so much that every time you engage in it you are not aware of how much time passes? I like to paint statuary. I open my windows, put on a favorite CD, have something cold to drink, and begin my painting. Hours later, I realize I am hungry and half of the day has passed by. I get lost in the art.

Find something you love to do and schedule time to do it. It could be as simple as a hot bubble bath surrounded by candles and a glass of sparkling cider. On the other hand, maybe long brisk walks early in the morning when most people are not up yet.

If you use a calendar to keep your appointments, actually mark a time in ink to enjoy your favorite activity. Make time for yourself. You schedule everything else, why not what is most important.

The activity I have chosen is: _____

I have scheduled some time on _____to enjoy it.

CHAPTER SEVEN

Harassment—Sand Box Tactics

There are laws on the books that are designed to keep you from being harassed because of gender, age, sexual orientation or race. What about supervisors who just don't like you? Currently the laws in the United States are very limited in this arena.

It seems you have more rights outside the work place than you do when you walk through your employer's door. It someone outside your work place followed you around and treated you the way many supervisors treat their employees, you could get a restraining order or some legal action against the person. When you are in the work place you seem to be a piece of furniture, or at least treated like it.

First, dispel any myths you have about being harassed. You did not earn it or ask for it. There was probably nothing you did that caused this reaction from your supervisor or "harasser." Many think they have done something or for some reason they earned this type of treatment. Not true. You have simply run into an individual who probably has never sought help for their personal inadequacies.

Like most Americans growing up, I was taught "if you work hard you get ahead." After years of loyal work to a large company, I came to realize that statement is not complete. One can still state a fact and easily mislead someone. You must learn to question half-truths. An example is advertising we see everyday. "9 out of 10 doctors prefer aspirin to other headache remedies" could be a true statement. However, do you know what the question was? It could have nothing to do with relieving a headache. Doctors could have been asked which product is better for thinning blood or helping with swelling. It is important that we do not assume the questions or an answer to statements made to us.

Another common phrase I hear comes from parents who say that children are extremely cruel to other children. One automatically assumes that these attics stay in the schoolyard. If you are reading this book you are painfully aware that it doesn't stop there. In fact, the harassment I witnessed and became a target of made me coin the term "Sand-Box Tactics." I could only image that the people who find a need to harass another person were the same kids in kindergarten who threw sand in other kid's eyes when they didn't get their way.

Unlike kindergarten, harassment can go on for a long period of time. An employee can be harassed for six months or several years. You are actually being targeted. A person who is harassed goes through a number of emotions. These emotions and feelings include, but in no way are limited to, feeling belittled, hurt, becoming unsure of themselves and their ability to do the job, frightened, fearful, and stressed. Physical signs can appear during the harassment or appear 6 months to 18 months later, after the harassment has stopped. Loss of weight, insomnia, stomach and digestive problems are some of the signs or results of being harassed. Panic attacks and post trauma syndrome (like many veterans must face) are also real results of being harassed.

This is very real. A person being harassed in the workplace has many life implications. Doubting your ability to function on the job jeopardizes your livelihood. We are talking about mental violence.

Other countries have already recognized that harassment in the workplace is a very important issue and have put laws on their books to reinforce action to be taken to prevent it.

In truth, it is still extremely difficult for an employee to file harassment suits against an employer even if the suit falls under our current law. To file a suit, an employee must have proof, factual information. Keeping an accurate journal and any additional proof (i.e., e-mails sent, memos, cards, letters) or witness statements, helps build and prove the case. Any employee deciding to file quickly learns the amount of money it takes to keep the case going. It is obvious the corporations have resources, teams of attorneys, to battle a single, less wealthy employee. These attorneys also know how to stall cases and keep them running for long periods, hoping the employee's resources run dry.

Coworkers still employed by the same employer are hesitant to get involved fearing for their own career. Unions can present false fronts when it comes to protecting their members. The Union does not exist if the companies aren't there. It's not unlike an umbilical cord.

What is unfortunate is that many times an employee who is being harassed ends up feeling very alone. Family members don't always understand what is taking place, if the person has even told family members. Many times a person who is being harassed becomes too embarrass to talk about it. Friends outside the company can be of great support. Even better yet, a former employee who has been part of the company, but has moved on. It is important to find someone with whom to share your experiences. You need to know that too many people in today's workforce experience use *sandbox tactics*.

Boot camp training—Exercise seven: Discover your myths.

As discussed in Chapter 2 we all carry with us different ideas or myths about the workplace. These myths keep us from getting ahead or help us in sabotaging our careers. More importantly, they keep us from seeing the work place as it really is.

Think about the myths you have heard and continue to carry with you. Exam them to see if there is any validity to them. Bring forward new ideas about the work place.

I used the example of the myth "work hard and you will get ahead." A person might think that means if I just do my job everyday and not get involved in office politics I'll get promoted.

Having a strong work ethic is good, but understanding office politics will help you get further. Taking risks also plays a part.

Now you try it:

MYTH #1 _____

Is it true? _____

How can I change this myth to make it better for my career.

CHAPTER EIGHT

Work Place Violence

Violence in the workplace costs industry over 4.2 billion dollars a year in lost revenues. Violence is the number one cause of death on the job for women and the number two cause of death among men. One needs only to watch the evening news to appreciate the severity of this modern-day epidemic.

With current headlines reading: "Sixteen Shot Dead By Disgruntled Coworker," and "Former Postal Worker Goes On Killing Spree," every employer must be wondering if they are next. Which employee will it be? On the other hand, will it be me? These concerns have shattered the American work place. Managers and employers can no longer ignore the importance of understanding their employees needs and perceived notions. The American workplace has become a crisis situation. No one is immune.

Larry Hansel went on a rampage after being laid off from his job. By detonating a series of radio-controlled bombs that he had rigged, Larry Hansel took lives of two supervisors.

A California father of seven, David Burke was fired from US Air. Several weeks later he boarded a plane that was carrying the supervisor that had caused his termination. With a smuggled .44 magnum, David Burke shot the supervisor, pilot and the co-pilot immediately after take-off. His actions that day resulted in the death of 46 people, including himself and 42 innocent passengers. This murder-suicide pattern is typical of disgruntled employees who seek retribution.

Arthur Knox had been passed over for a promotion. In a fit of rage he shot and killed three coworkers including his boss. In 1986, Patrick Sherrill had been reprimanded and warned he would receive a poor performance report. Dissatisfied with his review, Sherrill went on a rampage, killing 14 people at his place of employment in Edmond, Oklahoma.

Work-related homicide is now the third highest cause of death in the United States. According to a 1993 study by the National Institute for Occupational Safety and Health ("NOISH"), Americans experience 750 workplace killings a year, a number that is on the increase.

Table 1-1

	Executive Manager	Prof/ Specialist	Technical Support	Clerks	Mach Oper'tr	Labor
Homicide	0.90	0.26	0.12	0.18	0.20	1.48
Fall	0.32	0.14	0.19	0.05	0.35	2.16

On a monthly basis, approximately 90 innocent coworkers are killed, 3 to 5 managers/employees are attacked or killed, and 1 out of 10 employees have been harassed. These figures are staggering for the common workplace. Of these, the NOISH study found that out of every five victims of workplace violence, one is a woman.

Though that statistic sounds rather low, homicide in the workplace is the leading cause of death for women. During a recent airing of "America Close-up," News reporter, Mike Jensen, reported that, "With homicide now the number one cause of work related deaths in California, the state is searching for solutions."

Other states with high to moderately high incidents of place violence are Nevada, Alaska, New Mexico, Texas, Georgia, North and South Carolina, District of Columbia, Michigan, Kentucky, Illinois, Wyoming, Tennessee, Missouri, Arkansas, Mississippi, Alabama and Virginia. (NOISH, Aug. 1993)

Workplace violence is not limited to homicide. Beatings, serious injury, rape, harassment and other violent episodes are also widespread. There were an estimated 111,000 incidents of violence in the workplace in 1992 and these incidents cost employers and others 4.2 billion dollars. Acts of violence, which are directed against employers or former employers, comprise the fastest growing category of workplace violence, doubling, or possibly tripling, since 1989.

What does this mean to the American workplace? The Crisis Management Group in Newton Upper Fall, Massachusetts, estimated litigation costs due to violence in the workplace has increased dramatically over recent years. A lawsuit against an Austin, Texas frozen yogurt shop for the wrongful death of four employees recently settled for $12 million. A national retail outlet in New York currently has a $100 million lawsuit pending for the murder of an employee by a fellow worker.

An employer also needs to realize that one of four American workers has experienced harassment, threat of violence, or actual assault during the last year. Of these, fewer than half of the incidents of harassment, and only 24% of actual attacks are not reported

Company traits can make the atmosphere more fertile ground for these acts of violence. A company culture that ignores employees' complaints, management that treats employees disrespectfully, understaffing, chronic labor and management disputes, as well as an authoritarian management system all are characteristics of a troubled work environment.

Changing a company culture is a pain-staking task that can be defeated by managers who are opposed to change. Many companies do not think they need to change. "It is, however, difficult for corporate executives to believe it can happen in their own organization," states J. Branch Walton in his recent article "DEALING WITH DANGEROUS EMPLOYEES" (Branch, 1993).

Homicide in the workplace is the fastest growing crime of the 90's. Only one large company out of five has established a preventative program that deals with violence in the workplace.

Through my research, I have surveyed a number of employees regarding workplace attitudes. Numerous responses from these surveys deal with negative perceptions. These include being stepped over for promotion or statements reflecting a "why try" attitude. There were many comments about employees being fired because someone in management did not like what he or she said or did. Others held that lackadaisical attitude that a job at one company is just like any other job anywhere else.

Other reoccurring responses dealt with attitudes about upper management and perceived characteristics that employees feel management possess. These responses do not fluctuate much. "I can't wait until I get my time in and I am vested. Management here doesn't want to hear about anything they have to deal with," and "It's a job. Just don't tell anyone about a problem and it's okay" or "If managers had some backbone, this company could actually get work done right".

Time and again I have heard employees state that management sees any disagreement an employee may present makes that person (the presenter) a problem employee and a threat to the manager. They are not interested in solving problems but covering them up or getting rid of the employee who brought it to their attention.

When employees were asked what are the perceived attitudes management has towards employees and how do these attitudes play a role in the current motivations of their daily job responsibilities, many responses dealt with theories discussed in Chapter Five of this book.

The scientific method discussed how we, as individuals, use our senses to acquire knowledge. Real events are experienced and are perceived differently by each individual involved. An overwhelming response from employees held the belief that management at their company does not care about the employees and that management is more concerned with smoothing over the operations instead of improving their results.

Applying the cognitive theory (which relies on the basis that behavior is a function of a person's perceived beliefs and expectations) resulted with statements to the effect that employees do only what they need to do to fill an 8 hour work day. Since Management seems not to care about the employee, the employee does not care about the company.

The American worker does not seem to hold the attitude that hard work and effort would help promote their position. A result of current attitudes held by employees effect productivity and performance levels. Clement's article, HAPPY EMPLOYEES ARE NOT ALL ALIKE, (1993) provides information that shows employees can learn to be satisfied by producing less. Many employees throughout America have shown that they perceive their work goes unrewarded and that employees around them that perform and produce less get the same raises or even better promotions. Clement goes on to state that grievances are likely to increase as well as the numbers of those employees who chose to leave the company by quitting.

However, many employees I came across hold a belief that proceeding with complaints or grievances will cause management to brand them as troublemakers resulting in retaliation. This could decrease the numbers in grievances being filed and may not support Clement's research. In other words, employees do not report problem situations to management, but rather deal with these areas their own way. Hostile situations being one .

Using Lewin and Tolman's study, conclusions can be drawn that performance does not tend to improve by itself, but rather a change in motivation is the required stimulus to cause such change.

Violent behavior is linked to employees who carry a feeling of being powerless, unable to change the current working conditions and expectations of their jobs, stressed, and burned out (Supervisory Management Journal, 1994). This atmosphere harbors the violent acts occurring daily at workplaces and at schools through out the United States.

All is not hopeless. When asked what changes employers could make to improve an employee's outlook, employees named several options. Salary pay ranked among the lowest, while job recognition rated the highest. Applying the Expectancy Theory, measures a direct relationship with work effort and performance with rewards or recognition. When employees hold the belief that what they do and how they do it will directly reflect in their performance evaluation and be recognized, research proves that most employees produce at higher levels and are satisfied with their efforts.

A problem occurs when there is a discrepancy between the amount of working being performed and the amount of rewards received. The Equity Theory goes a step further to explain that employees will resolve this discrepancy by decreasing output and become less motivated to perform their job duties, when management does not intervene.

Repercussions can occur when employees feel their efforts have been neglected, when they perceive that they have been wronged (looked over for promotion) or victimized (retaliation for filing a complaint). These repercussions can take the form of hostility and violence.

In the October 1993 Personnel Management Association Journal, Richard Pascale states the management needs to be aware that disagreement is a vital part of a healthy organization. Pascale holds the belief that harnessing this contention constructively is managing the present from the future.

Better communication between management and employees without fear of retaliation is vital. J. Walton also states in his article "**DEALING**

WITH DANGEROUS EMPLOYEES," that management needs to listen closely and be aware of potential "Hot Spots." Roberta Bhasin states that managers need communication with their employees. They need to ask questions and review work habits.

Managers also need to be honest. A recent article in Drug Topics, 1992, states that no amount of money spent on employee morale can raise it when dishonest leadership can devastate it. Many employees believe that management is not honest in what they tell their employees.

Recognition for competence plays a large role in motivation and morale. W. Brown points out that condoning incompetence is one of the worst mistakes a manager can make.

James-Lange's theory proposes that emotions are experienced in sequence can be viewed here. The employee first approaches management with their problem in hope that there will be a mutual resolution. Upon finding out that nothing has been done or that they are now a target of retaliation, emotions such as fear, and insecurity can create a negative reaction. That reaction can be anger—and from anger spawns hostile and violent acts.

This violence may harbor in an individual for months or even years before erupting. The American workplace currently is a fertile ground for many more violent acts in the upcoming years if company attitudes towards employees remains as status quo.

Many employees have used their human resources department for complaints and felt the assistance they received was poor and extremely frustrating. Many do not realize that the human resources department in most companies is set up to serve the company. An employee's complaints are not confidential to the human resources person in which they have confided. Many times employee complaints are taken right back to the manager they may be complaining about. Human resources departments are advocates of the company, not the employee.

J. Stacey Adams presents in his Discrepancy Theory that human resources can play a larger role by evaluating and re-evaluating job requirements with pay and other terms when discrepancies are brought to their attention.

B. F. Skinner states that the Reinforcement Theory applies when an employee performs to the level of work desired by an organization, wherein a reward should match that behavior. Follow-through should also occur with those behaviors that produce lower performance levels than expected. Time intervals between reward and punishment play a large part in the effect of either. The shorter the time period between behavior and outcome the better the results.

Boot camp training—Exercise eight: Getting down to business

To help expand our career and make you more valuable to your company, you need to continue our education with classes and/or seminars. You could even take on a new challenge in your workplace.

Take some time to view this weeks employment ads in your local newspaper and see if you can find an area where employers need educated people. Computer experience has become a necessity for the new millennium.

Talk with someone in your human resources department who can review your current skill level and help point you in a direction to improve your skills. Then locate seminars or classes you can take. Smart companies offer many seminars.

My strong skills are: _____

I can improve my skills by _____

I can take a class or attend a seminar on: _____being offered at _____

CHAPTER NINE

What Can Your Company Do?

There are many things an organization can do to help prevent violent acts from occurring. These actions taken by companies cut the number of violent act dramatically, but cannot prevent all of them.

London, London and Mone theorize that organizational commitment, career satisfaction, and opportunity come before the work role. Belief in career commitment is directly related to skill and development. Companies who offer workshops throughout the year for employees and assist employees in attending an educational institution that will benefit the work environment are meeting this challenge.

The Grounded Theory is a theory based on goal setting and was developed by Edwin Locke . Here human resources departments' role can be expanded by assuring an employee's job and task performances can reach obtainable goals. By having human resources intervening in this manner creates a goal-oriented work force. Simply stated that achieving these goals gives employees' self-worth.

The Supervisory Management Journal brought forward in their recent article (June, 1994), the recent negligent hiring practices adopted by organizations are contributing to the increasing number of violent acts in the workplace. Steps need to be taken from creating a healthy company culture to improvement of supervisory skills. Measures to ensure conflict resolution as well as team building need to be in place.

A human resources department alone cannot provide the atmosphere required for a healthy, satisfied work atmosphere. Nor can every employee be adequately compensated for his or her perceived beliefs.

Companies need to spend time and money to develop a Violence Prevention Management Plan (VPMP). A committee should be set up which incorporates managers, employees, and union representatives and outside personnel who deal in violence prevention. This committee would be responsible for evaluating working conditions, employee beliefs and actual operations of the programs set in place to meet the needs of the Company and employees. The measures this plan should include are as follows:

PHYSICAL:
1) Survey the actual premises playing close attention to details such as high-risk areas, making them more visible. All areas should have good external lighting.
2) Locate areas where silent alarms could be installed for employee safety.
3) Increase the number of staff on duty in areas that may be prone to violent acts. Never leave one or two employees alone in a large office setting.
4) Provide bulletproof enclosures where needed.
5) Security should be more visible throughout the working day in high risk areas, not just gates or front doors.

EMPLOYEES:

1) Survey, on a company-wide basis, employee beliefs and current attitudes.

2) Survey employees as to requested job changes, resignations and firings.

3) Conduct training for employee's growth and improved skill levels.

4) Support employee promotion within their departments and make current job openings vital information for employees to obtain.

5) Offer classes that help promote employees, such as resume classes, dressing for the office. Treat these classes as a way to improve their current working situation. Offer these classes (for a certain time period) to laid-off or fired employees.

6) Develop an employee assistance program.

7) Follow-up questionnaire or interviews should be conducted on all complaints or grievances filed. Human resources needs to make sure a proper resolution has been reached with all parties concerned.

8) Create an Ombud's office, a place employees can go in full confidentially, to work through work place problems.

HUMAN RELATIONS and MANAGEMENT:

1) Hiring practices need to be written procedures that provide adequate evaluation of potential new employees.

2) Termination or complaints by employees need to be handled with respect and dignity.

3) All disciplinary actions taken need to be applied to each employee consistently.

4) Be honest in all matters. Stick to business practices and logical reasoning.

5) Listen to employees' problems and complaints. Follow through.

6) Observation: Be aware of an employee's drop in productivity. Warning signs can be seen when management is looking.

7) Confront employees with a genuine interest.

8) Spend time preparing. Know exactly what needs to be said. Be direct, concise and professional at all times.

9) Keep the employee informed. Acknowledge that their complaint has been heard. After an allotted time period, check back with the employee to see if an adequate solution has been met.

ON-THE-JOB:

1) Clearly state job duties and expectations.

2) Develop reachable goals for employees to meet.

3) Encourage an employee who presents a problem to present a solution.

4) Reward desired behavior.

5) Be consistent with expectations and follow through on statements and punishment.

6) Present workers with the model of behavior expected of them. Managers must behave and act according to their own rules.

7) Honesty.

8) Do not underestimate employees. They are keen and can pick-up on actions as well as talk.

PREVENTION:

1) Develop a written plan for handling potential violent acts or threats.

2) Immediate investigations need to be made on all persons who report a threat. All witnesses also need to be interviewed. Document all information in detail.

3) A specialist needs to be brought in to review potentially hostile/violent threats to employees and managers. This specialist can help determine if or what further action is necessary.

4) If further investigation is warranted, a team made up of at least human resources, security, legal counsel and management should develop a plan to develop and gather as much information as needed. This can and should include background checks, past

military service, weapons knowledge, and other predictors to violent acts.

5) Any investigation must be handled discreetly.

6) Interview the employee making the threat. Do not use any threatening actions or language. Be prepared with security measures if the employee becomes enraged. After interviewing the employee give them the rest of the day off.

7) Inform employee that before returning to the workplace, human resources will contact them with instructions. These instructions will vary based upon the decision made by the prevention team. If the employee is determined to be a threat, then termination may be chosen. Let the employee return to pick up their personal belongings after hours and under supervision. Counseling and referrals services may be an option.

8) Law enforcement and legal procedures should be looked into if the employee is an immediate danger to the company.

When an employee's frustration turns to anger, violence and hostility costs the workplace even more with the loss of human life. When a violent act occurs many people fall victim, property is damaged, employee's require time-off to confront their fears, hospital costs and benefits rise, and legal fees escalate. No one wins.

Companies cannot prevent the attitudes from the past, but can change the outcome of the future by implementing a number of measures found under the recommendations of this chapter.

An Ombud's office is one of the newest ideas companies have been embracing (listed as item #8 under Employees above). An Ombudsman has been proven to be the most effective concept to conflict resolution, and creates a safe haven for employees to resolve numerous issues.

This office is separate from any human resources department and would be the first line of contact. Human resources is a formal dispute resolution procedure. Many employees do not feel that human resources is fair, confidential, or even willing to hear their issues. Employee assistance programs deal with personal issues. An Ombud's office would traffic workplace issues by teaching employees and manager how to handle a variety of concerns and problems, while saving the company from high legal and arbitration costs. The Swedish parliament Ombud's office handles over 4,000 complaints each year. Of those over 1/3 are dismissed in the early stage of investigating the compliant without litigation.

The Ombud's office is an advocate of the workplace. Their goal is to bring forward fairness and safety for executives, employees, and companies who do business with your organization. Providing a safe haven for all employees to have their complaints heard, to be shown how to handle work place conflict, to provide resources when requested, and to assist in the full resolution of any founded problems. Adversarial relationships will lose fertile ground to grow.

The Ombud's concept is spreading worldwide. Some companies currently using this idea as successful tools are Eastman Kodak, Hewlett Packard, NBC News, UCLA, and Institute of Medicine in Washington, DC.

One such company, American Express, has seen great growth records in its net revenues. In 1996, the company saw a 12.6% increase and again in 1997 they had an 8.4% increase in revenue. For the previous twenty quarters, American Express stockholders have been extremely happy to hear that their company has met or exceeded their targets for earnings per share and return on equity.

I cannot help but believe that a happier employee base has contributed to this record and is the result of the wisdom of the company's chief officers.

If your company is not taking the upper hand on providing these safeguards or has ever considered any or all the suggestions made in the chapter, maybe you should. Be careful of suggestions you make. You must be politically savvy so your boss doesn't feel like you are trying to take their job, or your coworkers begin to think your ego has ruptured. For further information on presenting suggestions see chapter thirteen.

Draft a memo or letter to your chief executive officer. Tell them why these concepts are crucial to your company's success, explain how the company can save thousands of dollars in legal fees and lost productivity. If you do not feel you can include your name—do not. However, letters that are sent anonymously do not carry the weight of a signed letter. Be even more clever, by sending your CEO a copy of this book with a post-it note on these pages, highlighting this information. Those who stay silent are never heard.

Boot camp training—Exercise nine: Attitude is everything.

Have you checked your attitude thermometer lately? Companies are always looking for professionals with a "can-do attitude." It is widely known by recruiters that they prefer to hire someone with a positive attitude over someone who knows it all.

Keeping a positive attitude at times may seem very difficult. There are some attitude-destroyers to avoid.

Do not participate in idle office gossip that puts down your coworkers, company or department.

Do not feel sorry for yourself. Make sure that you remind yourself of the positive attributes of your job.

Do not compare yourself to other employees. Just because a coworker takes a two-hour lunch and is not reprimanded does not mean you should.

Do not talk ill of your manager to others outside your department, it will get back to them.

Think like a CEO. What would you like to see in the next person you plan on hiring for your company? List their traits:

#1_____

#2_____

#3_____

#4_____

How many of these traits do you have? _____

CHAPTER TEN

Changing Your Self Image

Ever see someone on TV and wish you could be more like him or her? There is something missing from the equation. You have no idea what that person may be thinking or feeling. Very often we assume that an individual who looks great and is smiling has everything they need or want in life. We do not consider the fact that they may be hiding fears or anxieties.

We are always surprised when someone rich and famous is found dead from suicide. We ask what could have been so overwhelming that their money or fame could not get them out. Often the answer is their mind.

Our mind is a strong tool that can make us happy or sad, feel hopeless or carefree. We teach ourselves many habits that are not easily broken. Hundreds of times a day we tell ourselves negative statements. These statements become our personal belief system.

Let's say you had to meet a client at a restaurant. Earlier in the day you wrote the name and address of the restaurant on a piece of paper. Just before leaving for lunch your supervisor comes in your office and gives you a new project with a short deadline. Now you're running a little late.

You rush off in your car and head to the restaurant. Suddenly you realize you left the name and address of the restaurant at the office. Not to worry you think to yourself, you have your cell phone. You reach for your phone when you realize the battery is low because the night before you forgot to charge the battery. What are you telling yourself right now? "You idiot! If you would have just taken the time to plug the phone in. Geez, you always get yourself in these types of messes. If only you were smart enough to think ahead." That is negative self-talk.

All day long we tell ourselves how we should think and feel. From the time we open our eyes until we fall asleep, we judge our actions and set our mood. Many phrases we use were placed in our thoughts from others as we grew up. Maybe a teacher told us we were a bad person, or a preacher said we were sinners. We may even believe we are bad people for merely becoming angry because we have been told that feeling this emotion is wrong. As young adults, we hold on to many things that were told to us, true or not.

AAA in my book stands for three lies we tell ourselves. They have to do with being angry, having anxiety and becoming an artifact.

Let's start with the latter. We become an artifact when we let fear of change and of taking changes keep us were we are. We tell ourselves we do not deserve better. Maybe we feel if we lost weight or changed, somehow we would be happier and get what we want. Yet we tell ourselves "I can't."

You are in control of what you think and how you feel. You allow yourself to be depressed or you make excuses for you behavior. For instance, you've had a bad day. How many of us feel it is okay to come home angry, avoid everyone, and shut ourselves off from the world? We pity ourselves—poor, poor me.

We can choose to say to ourselves: "Okay. Work, you have had enough of my energy today. I am going to have a great evening and not even think about you." You must change the way you think. Start taking notes of what you hear yourself saying. Is it true? Think of a better way of talking to yourself.

You may tell yourself you have a terrible job. The truth may be though I would prefer a position with higher status. I do not want to work the number of hours required to have the job. My job allows me more time with my family or it is very convenient to home.

You may tell yourself you have wasted your life and you will not amount to anything. This one seems to hit around forty years of age. The truth is that you are not wasting your life. You have the power to do whatever you chose to do. If you want a new career, you can take steps in that direction. Find out what you want to do. See if the company you currently work for has any openings in that area. Talk to the manager or director of that department. Ask questions. Determine what you need to do to reach your goal.

Do you tell yourself you do not have the ability to do a certain job or that you have no talent? Not true. I have yet to meet a person who does not have any talent whatsoever. Everyone has some form of talent. In 1999 a young lady who loved decorating hats decided she would take her talent and make it a business. No it was not your ordinary business start up. She ran her business out of her living room. By the end of 1999, she was doing over a million dollars of business. You do not have to be a Wall Street broker or have an MBA to be successful, just talent and tenacity.

Angry is a word many of us chose not to deal with. Is anger bad? Do you have a right to be angry? Do you then have a right to yell, scream and even throw things? On the other hand, is angry to be hidden?

Anger is not always bad. Your intentions can make it detrimental. If someone is attacking you or a loved one, you can become angry very quickly. It is an emotional response to stimuli.

If someone has honestly wronged you, you may feel angry. This doesn't mean you should start yelling and stomping your feet. Make sure you are not adding fuel to the fire. Have you held in previous incidents were you should have said something? Be careful not to become a boiler ready to burst. Are you telling yourself that matters are worse than they are. A case in point, someone at work keeps emptying the coffeepot and does not make more coffee. This has been going on for weeks now. Do you find yourself saying "it's so rude," or "who does that person think they are?" or "I'm getting tried of making the coffee—so I won't." Now you are angry and you have no coffee.

A simple solution—buy yourself an individual coffeemaker and keep it at your desk. Now you never have to worry about fresh coffee. You also have more alternatives. You can make tea or even hot cocoa if you want. Think creatively.

Anxiety rears its ugly head when you begin to fear something that does not exist. Many people have anxiety over getting in front of people and speaking. They are afraid that everyone will laugh at them. It this true? Will people laugh at you or do you think they could be sitting there feeling the same anxiety about their turn at talking? I am always amazed at coworkers who tell me they cannot speak in public. Just think about that statement. As kindly as I can, I point out they just did. Unless they are in their house, they are in the public domain. They speak in public all the time. So what is the difference? A state of mind.

Most anxiety comes from what other people may think of you. You avoid situations that make you feel anxious. This behavior may cause problems at work. Chances are there is nothing to be fearful about, or you are overestimating the danger or problem. You are already imagining a negative outcome.

Let's say you are giving a presentation tomorrow in front of the CEO and your director. What would be the things you may say to yourself? I am not a good speaker. I do not know the material well enough. My suit doesn't fit right, it's too tight. The video/slide/charts could not function properly and I will look stupid.

Let us just say everything you feared came true. Would you live? Of course. You could easily survive all those mishaps. What are the chances that all this would occur during your presentation? There is proof that you can set yourself up to fail. You could actually knock over the charts due to being so nervous. However, the likelihood that everything will happen is extremely small.

Place yourself in the audience. What would you think if you were sitting there listening to a presentation when a chart fell over? What would you do if the speaker made light of it and said something like "I said our profits where going up, not down"—you would probably enjoy it and love the break in a rather dry presentation. Managers love employees who can seize an opportunity and turn it to their advantage.

Women approach confrontation differently than men. Men are aggressive and competitive in nature. Women are connected and caring in nature. Both are needed in today's business world. When men have a conflict, they are more likely to forget but not to forgive. In other words, two men can have a yelling match in the morning and go for cocktails after work. Women, on the other hand, forgive and don't forget.

Men are visual and women are verbal. Men use their position to be more successful while women tend to use their position for security. It is important to understand the differences when dealing with people in the work environment. If you are a woman giving a presentation to an all-male audience, be visual and less wordy. To get your points across, use charts. If you are a man attempting to sell a woman CEO on a new product, use words that are more descriptive. Directly ask for her opinion on the product, then actually listen.

Even if you can control your emotions it does not mean you work with someone else who can. Often we are faced with dealing with someone else's anger. Don't become defensive or overwhelmed when it occurs. You have the skills to handle the situation. Be compassionate. Try to understand their point of view. The anger could be directed at you but not about you at all.

Don't let the situation intimidate you. Ask them to speak reasonably to you. Even try lowering your voice below your normal speaking level. Don't take the anger personally.

Now it is time to reward yourself. In an earlier chapter, you were instructed to get yourself something special. Something that made you feel good each time you look at it. In addition, you can immediately reward yourself all day long.

There are many ways you can give yourself a good feeling about yourself. Do something good for someone else. Take time out of your day and allow yourself to do something you had wanted to do. Maybe a coworker could use some nice flowers to brighten up their office.

Tell yourself when you have done a good job or when you did something right. Reward yourself by allowing time for some of your favorite activities. If you keep a calendar, write in the activity and block out time for yourself.

Boot camp training—Exercise ten: Self talk to yourself.

What do you unconsciously tell yourself which is undermining your self image? Think about it. Listen to the little things you tell yourself throughout the day. You may notice what you say when you look in the mirror in the morning and you hate the outfit your wearing. You may tell yourself you are not good at what you do simply because you make an error on a report or memo. These tiny sentences repeatedly said causes permanent damage. However, you are in luck. We can repair the damage.

It will not happen overnight, but you may be surprised at how fast it changes your outlook. You have been telling yourself these lies for years.

List what it is you say to yourself, then list the truth. Here is an example: I tell myself: I cannot do anything right. The truth is I do many things right. I love to share cards with friends to make their day brighter. I have good ideas on how to solve problems. I am good at volleyball.

Now you try it.

I tell myself: _____ The truth

is: _____

I tell myself: _____ The truth

is:_____

CHAPTER ELEVEN

It's Time For A Good Fight.

Have your boxing gloves on? Ready to go in the ring? That must mean that you have spent time exercising, learning the moves, and you know all the rules. Great. If not, them maybe you will want to read on.

The problem with fighting in the ring, there is only one winner. Fighting where it is a win-win-win outcome takes skill. There are certain rules to fighting right and fighting fair. Each principle is significant. Using these principals will get you what you need and keep your soul intact.

The same way a manager should treat you is the same way you should treat your manager when approaching a conflict. You need to be respectful. Name calling or hitting below the belt will not give you the results you need. Not communicating with the person you are angry at or have a conflict with is a lack of respect.

You may need time between the action and your discussion. It is not disrespectful to set up a time and place for this discussion to be held later. Not addressing an issue at all is insulting.

Make sure your problem or concern is not broadcast throughout your department. Whenever possible keep the conflict confidential. Only as you need to bring in others, do so. Always try to resolve conflicts in-house first. If you need to go to a supervisor, manager or even human resource department, do it after you exhaust the previous resources.

Approach all conflict with honor. Do not speak sarcastically but with sincere concern. Honesty is very important. Deception only leads to broadening the conflict. There is a certain humility which comes into play here. If you have accepted the fact that you have some responsibility with this conflict you are part of its cause. You can go further with humility than pride and get much more accomplished.

Obvious words and terms should not enter in the conversation. Words like *never* and *always* in themselves are false statements. Make sure what you present is unbias. This is why taking extra time before you address an issue you can think about what you are going to say and how to approach the situation. Do not attack or make accusations.

Solutions should not present themselves until the issue or conflict is fully discussed. If someone approaches you about a problem they observe, you should not attempt to solve it before they have finished expressing their concern. Otherwise, you will only present a partial solution since you have not heard the problem in its entirety.

You want the same respect. Make sure you get to present everything you need to present to be able to have a full and complete solution. If the person you are presenting the problem to does not listen to your complete presentation, then maybe a memo would be a better idea. You cannot interrupt a memo. Make sure that you include a possible answer to the problem after you have expressed your full concerns. Make sure your memo is presented in a clear and precise manner. Be careful not to babble or make a statement that is unfounded. Whenever possible, present fact and back it up.

If the topic you are going to address is of a sensitive nature, be careful. Protect areas that may trigger anger or a defensive retort. This is not the time to be getting "revenge." No one wins when the intent is negative. Harness your emotions and do not let your anger get a foothold. Once anger enters the conversation, you are on a downward gradual spiral that is uncontrollable. A few harsh words can cut deeply in seconds, but take days or weeks to heal.

When the other party does tell you their feelings or views, make sure you understand what they are saying. You must listen fully. In other words, you can not be thinking of what you are going to say next. Taking short notes can help you concentrate. After the other party describes their view, paraphrase it back to them. Tell them what you heard. For instance, if your coworker tells you that you have a tendency to take over a meeting with your suggestions while others do not get a chance to speak, resist the urge to respond with your ideas. Rather repeat back to your coworker what was just said to you, "Let me see if I understand what you are saying. You feel that I monopolize our staff meeting with suggestions while no one else gets to present their ideas. Is that right?"

What this allows you to do is: 1) think about what was said; 2) make sure you have it right before you open your mouth; and 3) let's the other person know you heard them. You are not saying you agree with them, just that you heard them.

You are the counselor. Realize that you may be teaching someone else how to handle a conflict in the future. That is right, you may be teaching someone something new. When you handle confrontation and conflict professionally, many people take notice.

Be kind to your adversaries. Pleasant words are healing to the soul. I am sure you can remember when someone you admired said something kind to you. For that matter, you probably can remember when someone you did not even know said or did something nice for you.

Boot camp training—Exercise Eleven: Thanks and Thanks again.

It's time to give thanks for the things we have and enjoy. Very often we forget there are things in our job and daily life that we actually enjoy.

Grab that pen and paper and let's get to work. Stop and think about the things at work that you do like. Some like the fact that their hours remain the same everyday. This makes life easier because they know what hours they are expected to work. Others like schedules that vary so that they can rearrange each week. Some people like a desk job so they do not have to brave the elements of the weather while others couldn't sit behind a desk if you had to tie them to it.

Now list those things you like on the job: _____

_____

_____

_____

Things I like at home: _____

_____

_____

Now post them somewhere you can see them daily. It is important to review these items daily. It reminds you that there are things you like about your job and home. When you learn to appreciate the good things, the things you value, the other stuff seems to fall to the wayside.

CHAPTER TWELVE

Negotiating

If you live in a world full of people, you must negotiate from time to time to reach mutually agreeable decisions. You probably negotiate daily. Maybe you want to go to a Mexican restaurant for lunch while your eating companion wants Italian. How do you resolve this issue? You can go for Italian today and Mexican tomorrow, or neither. Why not go for American Cuisine.

Developing these skills will help you be effective in the workplace. Proficient negotiators are successful in their field of work. Here are some basic tools for negotiating.

There are three very important components to negotiating. You need to have an eagerness to obtain information, be able to communicate well and solve problems. Information that you obtain prior to entering negotiations is what will make the difference between being successful and being a failure. You need to know the problem from all sides. You cannot afford to take a one-sided position. Gathering the information you require must start well before any negotiations take place.

You need to know each parties' position on the issue. Identify what they require out of the situation. Know if there are any timelines that need to be met.

Are the people involved in the negotiation individuals within the company that can make the type of decisions needed to solve the issue? Their personality will play a crucial part in the outcome. Become familiar with the way they deal with or resolve issues.

If you know of someone else who has dealt with the parties involved in the negotiation, talk to them about their experience.

List all the alternatives the other side has available to them. Having this knowledge will help you build a better option for solving the problem. The more options and alternatives you can have available the more power you will have at the table.

Develop a specific goal and plan regarding the outcome you desire. Prepare proposals that are specific, but that remain flexible. Know your bottom line.

Make sure your communication skills are clear and positive. This includes being a good listener. Make sure the discussion does not get off on unrelated topics. Focus on the problem at hand. Never lose your temper. Make sure both sides are engaged in the process of finding a positive outcome. Talk slowly and choose your words carefully.

Do not make threats or statements you cannot back up. Often individuals say "this is their last and final offer" when they don't really mean it. You lose credibility when you do not stand behind your words. It is very important to maintain a truthful stance bringing forward only those issues that are directly related to the concern or solution.

When you start the negotiating process, begin by presenting common values, viewpoints, and goals. Next, tackle the easier problems first. These require less effort and set a positive attitude for the more difficult issues.

Remember concessions will need to be made by all parties concerned. There is no place for blame or accusations during the negotiation process. Do not escalate the conflict. Knowing your bottom-line will let you know when you may need to step back from negotiating. Your bottom-line can change. What you want to avoid is getting into a deadlock position. Then it becomes a lose-lose situation.

If the negotiations become tactical or unruly, ask for a break or reconvene at another time. Set up the time and place right then. As the negotiator, reevaluate what took place. Why did a certain party act in a hostile manner. If possible, make sure certain hot spots are avoided in further negotiations.

You have not lost a negotiation just because you have changed your bottom-line. Make sure you are doing it based on information and possibly reconsidering your position. New information may have been presented to you during the dialog. Be patient and positive during the entire process.

When you as a negotiator can show the parties that conflict/concern is great significance to them and that outcome is of vested importance to them they will be more likely to make concessions. It becomes vital that a deal be reached.

Remember that you negotiate daily. You may use negotiations to solve a problem, to get a higher salary, or to get in a better position. If you feel you desire a pay raise and would like to approach your manager about getting one you would use the same tactics. First do your homework. Write out the job duties that you are performing. If there have been additional responsibilities given to you, make a special note of them. Make sure to include any classes or seminars you have taken to improve your skills.

A good time to discuss pay raises is during a performance review. Each and every performance review is a time to discuss your career, assess your skills, and encourage your manager to see that you are serious about your position within the company.

Anticipate what your manage may bring up. React appropriately to any criticism you may receive. Do not become defensive. Ask for more responsibility.

Make sure you know what your bottom line is when asking for a raise. If you have checked the market for the pay scale for you type of work, you will know what a fair offer is. Do not be afraid to turn it down. Give concessions that do not undermine your objective and your position.

Your goal is to leave with all parties feeling that they are better off having negotiated. A triumphant negotiator always makes sure they address all parties' needs, and do not focus solely on their own. A win-win situation is the best outcome of any negotiation.

Boot camp training—Exercise Twelve: Priorities.

Everyone needs to make sure their priorities are in order. Many times we loose track of what is really important to us. We start giving items precedence because of perceived deadlines. In other words, what task needs to be completed next gets all our attention. Most often we treat our nine-to-five job as being the most important aspect of our life but when asked most people will tell you it is there family that means the most to them.

Where does health, friendship, fitness, or fun rank in your daily activities? Do you make sure that you schedule time for what is important to you?

In any order, list those things in life you value most:

_____

_____

_____

_____

List those things you would like to accomplish:

_____

_____

_____

_____

Now—for a few moments look at both lists. From the first list, think about which item is most important to you. Then from the second list, which item you would most like to accomplish first. You may find some parallels between the two lists.

If you keep a calendar of your week's activities pull it out. If you don't grab your nearest calendar which you can write on. Pick a good day to schedule time for the activity or item you choose as you most important from the first list. Maybe it was quality time with your children. Wednesday you have no afternoon meetings. Ink in the time as an important meeting with a client and spend it with your children instead.

Many people feel guilty about using this time for their family or selves. Soon they realize they can give more back to the company when they have taken care of what is most important to them. Employees also find themselves less angry with diminished stress when they can have some kind of balance with their priorities and the company's agenda.

CHAPTER THIRTEEN

Office Politics

You have a new job. Congratulations. It's your first day on the job and you want to make a great impression. You wear your best suit, polish your shoes, and make sure your breath is minty fresh. You are given your new office and away you go.

Some of the most common mistakes in office politics are accomplished in the first couple of weeks of employment. One of the biggest mistakes is in forming friendships before you know who are the power players.

Put off becoming a part of a click or group of office workers until you have been able to figure out who your strongest alliances will be. Many times individuals are eager to recruit you for their cause or agenda. This doesn't mean you can't go out to lunch with someone, just don't go more than once in a couple of weeks time.

Meet as many people as you can as soon as you can. Schedule time to meet other office employees, no matter who they are. Instead of letting an office runner take your report to a boss in the next department, take it yourself. Use the opportunity to introduce yourself. Act as though you are running for political office.

Always be yourself, don't be someone you are not. People can see through false pretenses. Be genuine. We always love to be around someone we feel is being themselves. We know what to expect from them and we feel comfort in that.

Don't embellish your accomplishments. Let other speak for you. I am talking about not running around telling everyone what great work you did at your previous job or that you are an open heart surgeon when you were a front desk nurse. Keep it real. There are times when you need to toot your own horn, which is discussed later in this chapter.

Always remember compliments are appreciated when they are sincere. Phony compliments die quickly. Make certain that your coworkers and supervisors think you are a genuine individual. Remember that you can never replace the real thing.

Know the difference between professional gossip and office gossip. Getting caught up in office gossip can come back to haunt you. It is important to be seen as a team player. When you bad-mouth someone else others worry you do the same when they are not around.

Professional gossip lets you keep in touch with the inside track. Information, such as promotions, job openings, mergers, or what the competition is doing, is valuable knowledge you can use to further your career.

Make sure you don't just take in information. Professional gossip is a give and take relationship. You need to keep your lines of communication open. In addition, be careful of what information you use to gossip. If it is private—like you know a vice-president will be resigning due to cancer—you should leave out the private information and play dumb. Revealing personal information can be a detriment to your career.

Focus on your job at hand and be flexible. Remain positive. Make sure you know your deadlines are and expectations the manager has of you. If you do not understand a project, get clarification. There is no harm in making sure you are on the same track by repeating back to your manager what you believe is requested of you.

If you have been in the work place for any amount of time, you are already aware there is a lot of contradictions between what your boss says and what actually takes place. You may have heard that employees are valued or that a boss's door is always open when in reality the boss is never there or never has time. It is what a company values most that gets a majority of the attention. Many first-year business majors learn that companies value money, capital, and profits above all else. Get a hold of your companies yearly report and see where most of the money is spent. This will tell you what your company finds most important.

Very often good performances are not rewarded, just expected. When your review comes around it is no the time to be an introvert or John Wayne. Each review must be taken seriously. Performance reviews can be, and most often are, power plays.

First, you should always be aware of your company's policy. Know when to expect a review and be ready. Document your accomplishments. Keeping a 'to do' list can later be used to create an "accomplishments resume."

Make sure you list everything you have accomplished no matter how small. Even list those items you may feel weren't your best efforts. Bad situations can be turned around to show a positive outcome. For example, if you were suppose to be involved in setting up a task force for a new computer system by May and you finally got the system up and running in August, you may want to tell the company how you saved them money by postponing the initial installation until after the new fiscal year started as to avoid training and down-time at a particularly important time of year. On the other hand, maybe the delay allowed the company to buy the newest computer (since they are upgraded approximately every six months anyway) system on the market thus saving them time and money.

Do not put any weakness in print. Do not let a performance review have any weakness go in without your comments about it. If you have any negative comments on your review take the time to write your comments before signing the review. Do this immediately. Do not have your boss wait for days. Let them know immediately that you intent to write some personal comments and that you will have them to him or her by tomorrow. Keep your word.

Keep your comments to the point and make sure you do not come across as angry or childish. When you sign the form, make sure your comments are legible. If your form does not allow room to make your comments then attach them. Make sure the words "comments attached" is written on the front of your review so that there is no question you have submitted your own words.

Bad reviews can come back to stop you from getting raises or promotions. They can be used to point out weakness and faults.

The second reason to knowing your company policy on reviews is to make sure you get one and participate in it. Ally worked for a company for five years and never had a review. One day while talking to a friend in the human resources department she was told that reviews were done every six months. Ally was surprised. Her friend pulled her personnel file and found out that Ally did have reviews in her file, however not one was signed by her. In other words, her boss turned in the document without every giving Ally a chance to review his statements, five years worth. If Ally had been knowledgeable about the company policy, she could have asked her boss about her review when the proper time came. If she was not satisfied with his answer, she could have pursued it further with someone in human resources.

Be careful of making that big money saving suggestion. More often than not your suggestion will cause you big setbacks. Your supervisor does not like the fact that you are trying to take their job or make them look bad. You play a very tricky game when you want to present an idea. A politically savvy individual would make sure their boss is involved in the idea and gets shared credit—that is *if* your boss is willing to take the risk. Supervisors and managers often prefer not to be the focus of upper management. They have their little empire that is running just fine without a bright light concentrating on them no matter how good the idea.

Making a suggestion without getting your boss involved is just as deadly. Nothing is worst than an executive running in to your boss at a meeting and saying "Harrison had a great idea about X, Y & Z. It should save the company thousands." Your boss has no idea what the executive is talking about and stands there looking foolish. Not a way to build a good working relationship.

You pitch your idea and you are noticed. Your coworkers may see you as a show off and resent your becoming the talk of the town. Do not think for a moment that their ideas and feelings do not count for something. Someone you work with today could be your manager tomorrow. Building strong relationships on all levels are very important.

Never turn down the opportunity to do a favor that you may rely on later. Doing favors for people builds alliances. You don't have to like a person or have a personal relationship with them to have an alliance. The biggest example of that is the United Nations.

Be honest and earn respect. True power is when people will do things for you because you have asked them, not because you have placed the fear of God in them. When people know you play fair and are honest, you will be the person they turn to when they need help. You will be the person they trust.

Think about the people in your office who you would consider turning to in your time of need? What characteristics do you find them having? They certainly are not the people who will share your problem with the entire office. They are not the people who would stab you in the back two months later. Look closely at what they do everyday and why you chose them. There is a good chance they have their fingers on the pulse of the company.

Just because someone tells you something, don't believe it. There are a million backstabbers out there just waiting for the right victim. A coworker may encourage you to tell your boss that the way to improve his or her budget plan with your idea when in fact your boss hates input on his or her ideas. It would appear that your coworker is attempting to help you. Reality is they are setting you up.

You may find a coworker or boss undermining your abilities. They attack you personally or lay blame on you in an attempt to discredit your work. Never let your emotions get out of hand. You know your work ethic, do not let others tell you what it is. Step back for a moment and evaluate the situation. You may have to cut as many ties as you can with that individual without them realizing what you are doing. If you do not have to go directly to them, don't. E-mail instead of calling or meeting with them. You may need to refer to your E-mail later to prove what you said or did or what their response was. Avoid giving them any information they can use or turn against you. It could be as innocent as having a headache or feeling sick. Your backstabber could go tell the boss you are planning on calling in sick tomorrow. You never know.

If you are attacked, respond as quickly as you can. Take time to cool off first. Get your facts together then ask what the problem is and ask if they can give you more information. Maybe they have the facts wrong, feel free to offer an opportunity to correct this misunderstanding.

Remember our accomplishment resume? Use it. Promote what good work you have done.

Make sure the right people know what you have done and what you plan to accomplish. Keep people thinking positive about you.

Know your goals. Know where you want to go and how you are going to get there. Be flexible and allow these strategies to change as required. Companies get sold, down-sized or reorganize. The one sure thing you can count on is change. You must be able to bend with that change to survive. Your goals can change as well as your method of achieving them. Changing your goals does not make you any less of a person. Not having goals does. Be ready to offer your plans when someone who can help you asks. Those opportunities do not come often. You might not get a second chance.

Office politics is alive and well. Do not fool yourself in believing you can change companies or departments to get rid of it. Learning what the pitfalls are and how to avoid them is an acquired skill. Anyone can become proficient at maneuvering around bad situations.

Boot camp training—Exercise thirteen: What's Driving You.

Let's face it most people take the first job that comes along. It has been proven that most people do not work in the field in which they have acquired their degree. Why would this be happening? What drives people to take a job they did not study for nor have any passion for? It could be the fear of not having an income that drives them to these decisions.

How often do individuals stop and think about their decision? Are there better ways or alternative ways to acquire an income? Can you develop more than one type of income? Of course you can. Then why haven't you?

Stop and think about why you go to work everyday? Now write your answer:_____

_____

If you were fired or let go tomorrow what feelings would come over you?

_____

_____

What do fear most about your job? _____

How does this fear effect you? (Sleepless night, anger) _____

Are you a risk taker? Or do you play it safe? _____

Now look at your last answer. If you are an employee for a company and have developed no other income sources for your family you are a high risk taker. Many people believe a steady job is playing it safe. Think again. There are no steady jobs unless you create your own. It doesn't mean you have to start a company. Invest in stocks, invent something that will pay royalties, create a small home business using the Internet. Do something.

I will take a proactive interest in my well fair by looking into: Stocks Inventing Small Business

My deadline is: _____

CHAPTER FOURTEEN

The Golden Rules

The Golden Rule that many people refer to I have seen in many various forms. I have seen it written as "Treat others as you would have them treat you." I have also seen "The one with the gold makes all the rules." Of these two rules, which do you believe to be the smarter? Could it be that both are right? Can one out last the other?

This chapter will summarize some of the most important issues you should remember from this book. There are many ideas and concepts we need to work on daily to keep our lives in balance. Here are these ideas.

The job market has changed radically in the last decade. Our school system is still teaching our students, not how to think on their own, but how to follow direction. We are preparing our students to become employees and to continue the rat race. Good grades no longer equate to high paying jobs. Do not get me wrong. An education is one of your greatest riches. However, we need to get past the old myths and view our economic climate for what it is.

Many people are afraid to take risks with venturing out on their own. Yet, these same individuals work for someone else who can fire them on a whim with no plan B or second source of revenue (income). To me this is a very high to be living under.

Many people who work for someone else spend nights worrying about finances and job security. Their fear keeps them from being able to think past the moment to look into the future. Most people take the easier road. Night school, seminars, reading, or researching ideas that would create a better income is time consuming and hard work.

Silver Rule #1 Hard work performed by you for yourself will always pay you back.

You will get out of it what you put into it. Is it not better that you receive the benefits of your hard work than your employer? Spend time learning about a career that fills you with passion. Spend time thinking about new ways to build income. Spend time talking to successful people, the right people. Formulate other plans to support you then you will not be a needy employee and can rise above the everyday fears your coworkers suffer from.

Silver Rule #2 Learn. Learn. Learn.

Make sure you know yourself. Understand what you priorities are and how you can achieve them. Understand what things in life you value. Sharpen your skills. Learn to manage different risks.

Don't react without thinking everything through. Many times, we speak before we have had a chance to realize what is taking place. Be quiet for whatever time it takes to contemplate the problem at hand. Over reacting leads to further complications.

Do not always do everything the same way. Do not follow the herd. Just because everyone does it a certain way or makes certain statements, doesn't mean you have to follow the crowd. When you do that, you have a tendency to become part of the rat race. Other's negative comments begin to affect your life and your job.

Silver Rule #3 Do not become a target, dodge those bullets.

Bullies love targets and aim for them every time. Avoid the sand-box tactics. Speak up clearly. Have your facts straight. If you are attacked, fight back. Fight a good fight, fair and without anger. Always be professional. Always be positive. Keep an achievement resume on file. Use it whenever you need to present the good things you have accomplished. Never let negative comments go in your file without you presenting your information.

Silver Rule #4 Be ready to bend with the wind.

Change is constant. The workplace is a breeding ground for change. By its very nature companies must change and reinvent themselves to stay alive. Never become so set in your ways that you cannot change.

Do favors for individuals. Take on new tasks. Ask questions of other departments. Maybe you can help someone in another department by understanding how you job effects theirs. It could be as simple as not using staples in paperwork because they have to separate the work.

Silver Rule #5 It doesn't matter what you do, do something.

Be Different. You are not alone. There are millions out there like you. Companies are out to make profits and reward their shareholders, not to reward their employees. Too many people will jump at a chance to have a job, to get a paycheck, without considering what the real cost is for temporally relieving their fears. Companies pay workers that which workers allow them to pay. In other words, employees on a whole settle for less. Most people find themselves in a trap created, unfortunately, by themselves. Is it the employer's fault that they are living paycheck to paycheck, or is the employee relying and expecting too much from their employer. When you remove your dependency from your employer to depending on yourself, do you not become less fearful of what your employer may do?

Silver Rule #6 Be leery of what you are told.

Courtship deception occurs during the interview process. You're told the company promotes from within, employees are valued, reward systems are in place, and the boss's door is always open. You entire your new job with high expectations only to find out the words you heard do not match the actions of the company.

Or a coworker tells you that your new boss loves to have suggestions made about the way the department runs, when in reality she hates suggestions. Your coworker has just set you up.

Silver Rule #7 Communication and clarity can build friendships and stop bullies.

Make sure you have established good channels of communication with those individuals you report to and work with. Making sure an assignment is clear and understood will stop problems from happening later. It will also impede a bully from trying to say you did it wrong.

If you find you need to discuss a problem, don't hesitate to approach the topic. Do not react out of anger, be professional. Make sure you talk about the issue within a timely manner.

Silver Rule #8 If there is a problem, journal, journal, journal.

Keeping good and coherent records of what is taking place is of paramount importance. Date, time, what was said or done, any witnesses, are all vital information you may need to save your job. Be realistic and know what avenues you can and are willing to take to make your stand.

Golden Rule #1 Develop skills in negotiating, office politics, and work related fields.

Golden Rule #2 Always present a professional and positive attitude.

Golden Rule #3 Conflict is not always destruction, it can be constructive.

Golden Rule #4 Think. Think. Think.
The Platinum Rule: You can have a legitimate need, find a proper solution.

GRADUATION FROM Boot camp: Pat yourself on the back.

Congratulations, you did it. You have taken the first few steps in creating a better working atmosphere for yourself. You have a better understanding of the work environment. You are armed with new information, and ideas. Now you have to put them into play.

You can't stop here.

Keeping learning and growing. I have provided you with additional references and resources to help you meet your needs.

RESOURCES

Campaign Against Workplace Bullying (CAWB) a non-profit organization dedicated to raising awareness, lobbying for legislation, and offers support for individuals who have become targets. Donations welcome.

PO Box 1886
Benicia, California 94510
(707) 745-6630
Web Page: **www.bullybusters.org**

Crisis Management Group provides a unique program of professional crisis intervention designed to help organizations decrease post-traumatic stress reactions, enhance employee morale, strengthen confidence in management, and build the commitment of the individual and workgroup toward greater productivity.

381 Elliot Street, Suite 180L
Newton Upper Falls, MA 02164
1(800) 4447262
Web Page: **www.cmgassociates.org**

Contact Your Department of Fair Employment hears cases against employers. Find out if this department favors the employer or employee. You may have a rough time if your Governor and others supports employers. If that is the case they will probably rule in favor of your employer.

You may also contact the EEOC, Equal Employment Office. They are a different branch and handle harassment cases, too.

Write to your Congressperson, Senator, Governor and even the President and tell them you support laws against bullying. Other countries like the United Kingdom and Australia already have laws in place, protecting the workers. These addresses can easily be found on the web.